HORIZON

JULY, 1963 · VOLUME V, NUMBER 6

HORIZON

A Magazine of the Arts

JULY, 1963 · VOLUME V, NUMBER 6

PUBLISHER
James Parton

EDITORIAL DIRECTOR
Joseph J. Thorndike, Jr.

EDITOR
William Harlan Hale
MANAGING EDITOR
Eric Larrabee
ASSOCIATE EDITOR
Ralph Backlund
ASSISTANT EDITORS
Jane Wilson
Albert Bermel, Shirley Abbott
CONTRIBUTING EDITOR
Margery Darrell
EDITORIAL ASSISTANTS
Caroline Backlund
Wendy Buehr, Priscilla Flood
COPY EDITOR
Mary Ann Pfeiffer
Assistants: Joan Rehe, Ruth H. Wolfe

ART DIRECTOR
Irwin Glusker
Associate Art Director: Elton Robinson

ADVISORY BOARD
Gilbert Highet, *Chairman*
Frederick Burkhardt   Oliver Jensen
Marshall B. Davidson   Jotham Johnson
Richard M. Ketchum   John Walker

EUROPEAN CONSULTING EDITOR
J. H. Plumb
Christ's College, Cambridge

EUROPEAN BUREAU
Gertrudis Feliu, *Chief*
11 rue du Bouloi, Paris

COVER: In 1527 Sir Henry Guildford sat for the painter Hans Holbein the Younger, who had just come over to England from Basel. The result confirms David Piper's observation, in his book *The English Face*, that "Holbein seems to have that purity of style through which a sitter appears to tell his own story, with a clarity that is a distillation of the truth." Guildford was a man of parts, a friend not only of Henry VIII but of Sir Thomas More, and an acquaintance—or at least a correspondent—of Erasmus. His superb portrait is now in the British royal collection, which is described by Oliver Millar, Deputy Surveyor of the Queen's Pictures, in an article beginning on page 92. (Reproduced by Gracious Permission of Her Majesty the Queen. Copyright reserved.)

FRONTISPIECE: One false move and a glorious human pyramid will land ingloriously in the middle of the Grand Canal in Venice. This gymnastic feat was performed by fifty men, of the Castello and San Nicolò quarters of the city, atop two gondolas on January 19, 1806. It celebrates the signing of peace agreements between these traditional rivals six years earlier, when mutual distrust of their new Austrian rulers had finally united the citizenry. Such human formations recall those actually used to scale the walls at Aquileia in 1420, by both the Castellani and Nicolotti factions, when that city fell to the Venetians. The early 19th-century engraving is by Ignazio Columbo.

Philadelphia Plain & Fancy

An aristocracy of Old Families, Quaker in conscience if not in religion or taste, still swings its weight in the business, social, cultural, and even the civic life of Penn's "holy experiment"

By NATHANIEL BURT

There used to be a time when people didn't really believe in Philadelphia, especially in the twenties and thirties and in New York. Of course they knew there was such a city. They sometimes passed through it on the train. Otherwise it was just a statistic. When people heard stories of the kind of thing that still existed there, they didn't like it, and refused to accept it. Typical was the reaction of one of the more brittle female members of New York's Algonquin group. Caught by mischance at a Philadelphia dinner party during the thirties, she went around muttering "Moss, moss on everything!" Certainly Philadelphia between the two world wars did lie across the path of the roaring twenties and the sophisticated thirties like a big black fossil. It was neither exciting like Manhattan, quaint like Boston, nor

If there is one citadel of Old Family influence in the modern city, it is the Philadelphia Club, the country's oldest. And if there is one man who deserves the title of "Mr. Philadelphia," it is Edward Hopkinson, Jr., seen on the facing page in the club library. A descendant of Francis Hopkinson, the Signer, he is a senior partner of Drexel & Company and former chairman of the Philadelphia City Planning Commission.

picturesque and glamourous like the South and West. It was not even conspicuously awful like the Midwest. It was just there; and so, safely ignored.

But then came *The Philadelphia Story* and *Kitty Foyle* and Grace Kelly, a true-life princess who must have been brought up in a magic tower of some kind. Philadelphia, it seemed, really did exist after all.

Not that the first impact of Philadelphia is one of shining princesses and magic towers. Rather it is one of sprawling dinginess, with a skyline whose highest building remains the great marble City Hall, completed in 1904. Philadelphia is there all right—America's fourth largest city and second (though inland) seaport, founded by William Penn in the name of God as a refuge for a persecuted religious sect, inspired by Benjamin Franklin's dream of the Enlightened City, the young Republic's first capital, shaped by the conscience of Quakers (the Plain) and the tastes of their rich Episcopalian descendants (the Fancy), devoted to moderation but fond of good living, a puzzle to strangers, a Hidden City whose charms yield only to long and careful exploration.

The arriving stranger commonly brings with him two preconceptions, two highly developed Philadelphia myths. These

This is the city that Benjamin Franklin saw when he arrived at Philadelphia in 1723, landing from a small boat at the Market Street wharf

might be labeled the "Dead Burg" myth and the "Fox-Hunting Aristocracy" myth, the one the idea that Philadelphia is utterly lacking in gaiety, a town of Quaker slowness and sobriety; the other that it is the citadel of an extremely frosty upper class almost wholly devoted to snobbishness and horses. Like many myths, both are based on solid fact.

There is no doubt, for instance, that Philadelphia has one of the least rewarding night lives of any city in the world. It is an axiom that Philadelphia has "no good restaurants," and that its *boîtes* are as lively as wet flannel, its theatre spotty and secondhand. It is not Fun; it is the Salesman's graveyard.

The second myth is true also. There is very definitely a fox-hunting gentry in Philadelphia, and Philadelphia really is a center of fox hunting. However, there is not much evi-

dence of this on Broad Street. No pink coats are worn there, and in fact there is not much visible evidence of the existence of any kind of gentry, fox-hunting or otherwise. One sees well-set-up, well-dressed, outdoorsy gentlemen coming out of offices at noon and at five, but then, no more than one sees on Wall Street or State Street or Michigan Avenue. There is a definite lack of the chic matronage one sees on Park Avenue or Lake Shore Drive. There is in fact no really "smart" shopping section or residential area. "Smartness" is just what Philadelphia deliberately avoids.

This does not mean however that the gentry don't exist, or even that a good many of them aren't smart, after their fashion. Their comparative invisibility in town can be accounted for in at least two ways. For one thing, there are so few of them. The Social Register lists, out of a metropoli-

A bronze statue of Washington looks down Benjamin Franklin Parkway to the tower of City Hall, itself topped by a statue.

...ter Cooper's painting shows the homes, stores, and commercial buildings of the rich Quaker merchants, strung along the ship-filled Delaware.

tan area population of more than four million, no more than thirty thousand individuals (but more than any other city except New York). This is less than 1 per cent of the total population; of these only a fraction would be acknowledged as really upper class by Philadelphians themselves.

But even more important than sheer lack of numbers is the fact that nearly all the gentry, in a proportion of ten to one, live out of the city and prefer to stay there. When approached by a stranger in the perennial American game of "where do you live?" a young matron is likely—like the girl being presented at the British Court when asked by the Queen where she lived—to reply simply "The Main Line." It is often a great surprise to Philadelphians to realize that other people sometimes don't realize not only where but what a Main Line is. The Main Line is, of course, the main

The Anatomy of an Aristocracy

The text of this article is drawn from the pages of a forthcoming book, The Perennial Philadelphians: The Anatomy of an American Aristocracy *by Nathaniel Burt. Son of Struthers Burt, whose books on Philadelphia are still regarded as the best portrait of the city, Nathaniel Burt is himself a part of Old Philadelphia, although he now resides safely out of reach in Princeton, New Jersey. His book, to be published by Little, Brown & Co., will do for Old Philadelphia, in more detail, what Cleveland Amory did for Proper Boston.*

...that lofty marble perch the Founder can still see over any building in the city, including the big blocks of new apartments at the right.

line westward of the Pennsylvania Railroad, and it is odd but true that a great many of the Philadelphia fox-hunting gentry live along its tracks.

None the less, despite the small numbers, deliberate un-ostentatiousness, and distant residence of this gentry, a curious and contradictory observable fact is that there are no streets in America where the gentry, when they are seen, stand out with such striking and sore-thumb obviousness. In Boston everybody takes on a Proper Bostonian look. In New York the real gentry are lost in the crowd of people trying to look like Somebody, and succeeding. In Philadelphia people tend to look exactly what they are; it is the only city in America, for instance, where the lower middle class looks exactly the way a lower middle class is expected to look. Here, as in England, the streets are full of slightly anemic, slightly crushed, rather neatly and badly dressed but, at the same time, very respectable and overwhelmingly self-satisfied people who one feels are thoroughly smug about the condition to which God has called them. Standing out from these, one sees occasional people of an obviously different, and again obviously native, race—taller, often handsomer, usually healthy with bright cheeks and sound teeth, well dressed in a somewhat careless and tweedy way, but one with the lower orders in that same supreme satisfaction with things as they

are. A fascinating spectacle is the calm natural aplomb of a Philadelphian strolling along the street in an off hour quite sure that Nobody Else is there.

Both this comparative absence and curious conspicuousness of the gentry on the streets of Philadelphia are significant. For this is a city that has been owned by and managed *for* (not *by*) one of the few, if not the only, still-established hereditary oligarchies in America, perhaps in the Western world; certainly one of the few whose tenure extends without any real break from the early eighteenth century to the present; a tenure however that has tended to become more and more, until just very recently, an absentee landlordship.

The stamp of both the presence and absence of this owning oligarchy is everywhere visible. Take, for example, the disreputable, snaggle-toothed obsolescence of so much of Philadelphia's real estate. This is traceable directly to the fact that the owners and administrators of it live elsewhere, immune from city taxes and politics, shielded from the sight of what their absence has done to the basis of their fortunes. A half-century of neglect is bound to show sooner or later.

Or take, on the other hand, Philadelphia's assets: the grand gestures, the public monuments, each one bearing like a thumbprint the impress, usually, of some one prominent Philadelphia family; the Free Library, spiced with statues

8

Philadelphia has always prized good parties and lovely hostesses. Its social life reached a peak of elegance in the decade after the Revolution when Mrs. Anne Willing Bingham (at right in a Stuart portrait) reigned as the queen of a social "court" which John Adams, for one, thought altogether too grand for the young Republic. It reached its peak of ostentation in the early twentieth century when Peter A. B. Widener built Lynnewood Hall, a marble palace the foyer of which appears opposite. Entertaining is quieter now. One of the leading hostesses is Mrs. Emlen Etting, whose portrait (above) was painted by her artist husband.

and portraits of Peppers; the Franklin Institute, Philadelphia's museum of science, of which one of the proudest exhibits has been the Bible of the Duane family, descended so casually from Benjamin Franklin; or the Academy of Natural Sciences, where stands pre-eminent a large habitat group that includes a moose shot by a Biddle and stuffed by a Cadwalader. Every church, every museum, every public building, reveals sooner or later the traces of these patrons and benefactors, most of them Old Philadelphians, all of them enshrined somewhere by a plaque or a bust or above all a portrait. As inevitable as fountains in Rome, in any business office, school, or hospital, one is likely to find this shrine to the Founding Fathers—the portrait and the grandfather clock and usually, to complete the grouping, an eighteenth-century chair. If you wanted to make for some Academy of Human Sciences a habitat group of a stuffed Biddle or Cadwalader, this would certainly be the setting—portrait, clock, and the appropriate specimen sitting in the chair.

The back-street charms, the trees, the few nice streets of old houses, the unexpected little gardens, public and private, all the things that make for that tucked-away, elusive "Philadelphia charm" are entirely the residual traces of its gentility. The minute you get beyond the central citadel, North of Market, South of Pine, all this disappears.

Even the city's ambitious new redevelopment program is motivated to a large extent by a rebellion against old corruption and a change of heart within the ranks of the gentry itself—a realization that absentee landlordship and delegated politics were leading to ruin, and a valiant effort, led by a member of the gentry, Mayor (now Senator) Clark, to lift Philadelphia out of a depression caused largely by the lack of aggressive and up-to-date Old Philadelphia leadership.

The Old Philadelphia gentry is then, at most, still the real owner and ruler of the city; at least, the drop of Tabasco that gives character and flavor to the whole. It is certainly, by either presence or absence, a very important factor, perhaps the most important single factor, in the life of the city.

No one, of course, is more serenely aware of this than the Old Philadelphian himself. This awareness may be hidden under layers of careful indoctrination, a rigorous training in modesty, cordiality, and relaxed, cheerfully casual good manners. But buried under it all, like the Church's One Foundation, lies a subconscious veneration for his own Position. It is the fact of this venerable Position, into which he is born and to which he must react in one way or another, that largely determines the upper-class Philadelphian's attitudes and career. He can take advantage of it or escape it, love it or loathe it, maintain it or rebel against it; but it is *there*,

TEXT CONTINUED ON PAGE 12

OVERLEAF: Elfreth's Alley, claiming to be the oldest continuously inhabited street in the U.S., looks about as it did in Franklin's time

TEXT CONTINUED FROM PAGE 9

like Philadelphia itself, and as long as he stays in Philadelphia, he's in for it. Whether he likes it or not, he will be enmeshed in a sense of belonging at once cosy and asphyxiating. He can run away to New York, Paris, or out West, but a place will be kept for him at the table, and his foreign-born children can come back and find a vacancy waiting there like a seat in the family pew. "People know who he is," as Philadelphians would put it.

Actually all but the most liberated of these people consider themselves, and refer to each other, not as "Old Philadelphians," of course, but just plain Philadelphians. *The* Philadelphians. When they refer to someone as a Philadelphian, they don't mean for a minute just any one of the city's four million residents. They mean one of their thousand friends, connections, or relatives. As far as they are concerned, there are no other real Philadelphians and there is no other real Philadelphia except those particular areas where these particular Philadelphians live or have lived. The rest of the city is terra incognita, a something that surrounds the real city like a natural phenomenon, a forest, or a swamp.

Although these Old, these Inner Philadelphians are certainly a distinct tribe, it is not so easy to pin down the characteristic markings of the species; and in fact that very lack of the characteristic is part of the characteristic. There is, first of all, the tradition of Quaker camouflage, the avoidance of show either in worldly goods or in unseemly emotions; then there is the Anglican tradition of avoiding what is Bad Form. Besides these two negatives, there is a general tendency toward withdrawal, hiding away, saying "No" to the rest of the world. What Owen Wister called "the instinct of disparagement" that makes Philadelphians habitually run everything down, especially things Philadelphian, is a form of this negative. This has the advantage of modesty; it also is a blight on creative effort, on reform, on any new enthusiasm. It pervades the air of Philadelphia with a sort of communal shrug, an indulgent laughter that has its charms but can be disheartening to the intense—as it is meant to be.

It is perhaps, too, in negatives, in the places and peoples Philadelphia is *not* like, that Philadelphia can most easily be bracketed. It is, for example, *not* like New York. Certainly no two large cities, so close together, could be more different. If Philadelphians can be said to be self-conscious about anything, it is in their desire not to be like New Yorkers, or what they think of as New Yorkers. This is more than mere antipathy; New York is too close, and represents too strong an economic threat to be ignored as Philadelphians would prefer to ignore it. It represents too easy an escape for the rebellious, talented, ambitious youth who has opportunities there he cannot have at home. From the point of view of the Stock Exchange or the theatre, Philadelphia is just a suburb. Philadelphia women go to New York when they want to buy clothes, and their men when they want to buy women. There is an element of uneasiness in having the world's largest city on one's doorstep.

New York represents serious competition, but Philadelphia is damned if it is going to compete. The whole aspiring,

The city has begun an ambitious program to restore its blighted areas. This is part of the once-fashionable Society Hill district as it looked in 1960, with St. Peter's Church in the background

pushing, ostentatious, inhuman, showcase quality of the city, the raucous glitter, the avidity for the novel, the insistence on the high pitch, everything about it in fact rubs Philadelphians the wrong way. Put a "Not" in front of any of these New York characteristics, and you get a Philadelphia one.

In all this, Philadelphia is one with New York's more distant northern neighbor, Boston, and it would seem that these two would have much in common. Both Philadelphia and Boston are comparatively old-fashioned cities, both dominated by local aristocracies, both given to good works and antiquarianisms. They are both of the same coin, all right, but with opposite faces; almost everything that is true in detail of Boston is untrue of Philadelphia. There has been a neat comparison in the cities' respective Athenaeums that illustrates the conflict of the two places on such subjects as books and food. First of all, they both have Athenaeums. These are private subscription libraries to which one has to belong, usually by descent, as a "shareholder." And both do contain books; here the resemblance ends. The Athenaeum in Boston is a thriving affair, busy with researchers from Harvard, its every nook and cranny thick with learning, if not necessarily shareholders. When it offered refreshment, as it did until recently, the fare was Spartan: tea or bouillon was served, with three plain crackers, for three cents; cheese cost two cents more. Each additional sweet cracker was an extra penny. Lately even such orgies as these have been discontinued.

The Philadelphia Athenaeum, which occupies a stately high-ceilinged brownstone building on Washington Square, is comparatively empty. But once a year the shareholders turn out for the Athenaeum lunch. After passing through a

This is the adjoining block in 1961. Slum buildings like those seen in the facing picture have been torn down, leaving a row of historic houses, now refurbished, and a new small park.

receiving line of patronesses, they listen to a speech calculated to salve their consciences and whet their appetites; then they set to, on a feast of turtle soup, pressed duck, spoon bread, tomato aspic, and meringue cake, after which all leave quickly so as not to be caught by their more unfortunate relatives. The cause of Literature has thus been served for the year.

Hating New York, unacquainted and basically unsympathetic in some ways to Boston, ignoring the Midwest, Philadelphia—the Philadelphia of the Old Philadelphians—does look with kindness upon two sections of the globe, the South and England. Links with the South have always been very strong, and Philadelphia regards Southern ways, that is Old Southern ways, with somewhat the same mixture of envy and disapproval with which no doubt the Prodigal Son was regarded by the boy who stayed home. The South is the black-sheep cousin, reckless, ruined, but oh, how romantic! A Southerner with good connections is almost sure to be welcomed with open arms, and the best marriages have been made from the earliest times across the Mason-Dixon Line with Virginia Lees and Charleston Middletons.

Philadelphia admired and still admires nothing more than the South's landowning patriarchal quality, the horse raisin' and fox huntin', the lavish hospitality, the fragrance of belles and juleps, the high-minded disdain for mere mercantilism. But alas, Philadelphia cannot approve. Disdain of mercantilism is one thing; recklessness and shiftlessness are another. Having a good time is delightful, but being a wastrel is something else again. Common sense, caution, and the Quaker conscience have to count in the end.

As for England, that other land of the Old Philadelphian's

heart's desire, it has the inestimable advantage of not being American, and hence pleasantly removed from the actual concerns of this world. The England that Philadelphia loves is, of course, never, never the England of Birmingham, which Philadelphia most nearly resembles, but a sort of Gilbert and Sullivan England, or the country, more or less gone in fact, that is imperishably preserved in Trollope.

In many ways Philadelphia remains exactly what it used to be: the second largest city of the British Empire. In its flatness, its monotony of row houses, its grim industrialism, it is as English as can be. In the love of country and country values cherished by the upper classes, and in the equal cherishing of the upper classes by themselves, it is also English. In all sorts of traits of English descent, from a style of blond good looks, negligent arrogance, and casual high living derived from eighteenth-century English inheritance, to a rather fundamental trust in a sort of Establishment of Church, Government, and Culture presided over by the aristocracy, Philadelphia is very like an antique Toryish England—the England perhaps of Galsworthy, and nothing whatsoever to do with the England of Aldous Huxley, Bernard Shaw, Harold Laski, or Evelyn Waugh.

But though they cuddle illusions of English superiority in taste and manners, Philadelphians are happy to admire England from afar. When it comes down to brass tacks, as it did in 1776, they are not going to give up any local perquisites, or take any guff from the Lords Proprietor. For the English visitor of rank or charm nothing is too good; but woe to the Bishop who, on a memorable occasion, began his lecture, "I take it I am addressing members of the middle class."

As perhaps the only hereditary gentry outside of Kuwait and Afghanistan still mounted, however shakily, in the saddle, Philadelphians can afford to smile gently if complacently at those lovely, charming, impoverished Southerners, those pushing, overstylish New Yorkers, those odd, bookish, Irish-dominated Bostonians. Even the English nobility, groaning under the yoke of the Welfare State, draws from the Philadelphia eye the sympathetic, but yet a bit condescending, tear.

Perhaps the nearly three-hundred-year-old reign of this Philadelphia family group, this continuous web which continually weaves in new strands, is coming to an end. A revolution has certainly occurred; but to a great extent, Old Philadelphia leads it. All sorts of new blood and new power have come up, but not yet to submerge Old Philadelphia in its financial, cultural, or even basic political primacy. Certainly not in its social primacy.

It is almost impossible to exaggerate the thickness of identification that an Old Philadelphian has with this city. Imagine an unlikely scene: a Very Oldest Philadelphian strolling around the edge of City Hall, and connecting his Family with what he sees. City Hall itself might have few such connections: a couple of ancestors in white wigs in the gallery as portraits of long-dead mayors, others on the walls of the Law Library there. Another more recent, less often mentioned ancestor made his out of the marble of which City Hall is

built. Around the base of the pile are a few statues to nineteenth-century connections, generals, reformers. North, up Broad, he sees nothing but the Academy of Fine Arts, where more ancestors hang, and of which innumerable forebears have been directors. The same is true of those pillared institutions along the Parkway (more portraits, more patrons), especially at the Art Museum, where his sisters and his cousins and his aunts are still all patronizing donors and committee members.

Out there sits the equally neo-classic station of The Railroad (the Pennsylvania, naturally), to which the family contributed those directors (only in the right decades, of course). Southward lies the world of banks—the Girard, the Provident, the First Pennsylvania. His wife's grandfather was president of one, his brother-in-law's uncle is chairman of another. That skyscraper there bears the family name; this one was designed by a cousin in love with the Colonial. Farther south comes the Union League (most of the family, except the most distinguished and Democratic branch, have been members from the beginning) and the Bellevue, scene of infinite balls and Assemblies, and the Academy of Music (every single woman in the family has spent every single Friday afternoon there for every single winter). To the east spreads the Delaware, on the banks of which the family had

its first houses and warehouses; to the west, the Schuylkill, where in later generations bloomed their country seats. As he looks about him and sees each landmark starred with conspicuous family associations, how can he help but feel identified, important, elevated into Position? This is His City.

It has been "his city" since 1682, and though the oligarchy has had its ups and downs, it has never been down and out. Philadelphia and the oligarchy stand now in the hope of a new wave. Will history repeat itself? In the ten years before 2000 will Philadelphia achieve another climax to match those of 1790 and 1890? Of what kind? And will this city of 1990 still be His City? These questions definitely ferment in the mind of the more intelligent Old Philadelphian. But most of the time he continues to jog along in the comfortable ruts laid down for him by his ancestors; no longer so comfortable, but still ruts: law, medicine, insurance, banking, good works, institutions, clubs, sports—even the arts.

Along these ruts there is much that is worthy, curious; even, in a smothered way, great. Great men, most of them now unknown, have made the ruts, created the institutions. Great things have been done in the city, most of them forgotten. Philadelphia is quite willing to have it that way, and stay Hidden. In a sense Philadelphia is not the past but the future. Philadelphia is what cities *become*—all those other cities that once, too, hoped to be Number One, and find themselves growing older, like Philadelphia, as Number Two, Number Three, Number Four. Better then to be oneself than Vulgar Number One.

Philadelphia is now hopeful again; but its inhabitants, perhaps more so than those of most American cities, are inclined to be unillusioned. The ruts are comfortable and secure, but they do not lead to the stars, to the Bonanza, to the Championship Cup. Philadelphia had the Cup, and lost it, and is now used to making Madeira out of sour grapes. It's a fine vintage, warm, rich, flavorful; but there's a drop of bitterness in the bottom of the glass. Philadelphia has, after all, for all its prosperity, been a Disappointment: not the Holy City Penn had in mind, not the Enlightened Center of the Republic Franklin had in mind.

It has been something else, maybe worse, maybe better. It has been—well, Philadelphia.

The Old Families:
What's Better Than a Biddle?

Nicholas Biddle, Jr., descends the steps of his great-great-grandfather's Bank of the United States, once the country's center of financial power, now a museum. Mr. Biddle is an insurance broker (Biddle, Townsend and Company), and Republican candidate for Commissioner of Lower Merion Township.

This hallful of Biddles turned out for the family's 250th anniversary in 1931. The family reckons its founding from the arrival in New Jersey in 1681 of William Biddle, a Quaker shoemaker whose descendants moved across the river to Philadelphia. Greatest of the tribe was the fifth-generation Nicholas, presi-

The ideal Philadelphia in-group, the group Philadelphians above all prefer to be in the middle of, the ultimate club, is the family; not the immediate family circle but the total family of in-laws and connections—"kin." In fact one can almost say that all the functions of upper-class Philadelphia life are conducted as though they were family gatherings, family councils, family festivals. The tone of good-humored, relaxed chumminess which Philadelphians prefer is exactly that of a merry family Christmas party, where everyone knows everything about everyone, and there is nothing in the atmosphere that cannot be taken for granted.

This standard applies anywhere. Business is to be conducted as though a family council were managing the estate, with the help of family lawyers. Pleasure consists in clan meetings. Whether at small dinner parties or at massive teas or

at informal gatherings in local country clubs, the ideal of a family group coming together to celebrate its mutual affection and self-esteem is basic, no matter how diluted by suburban dispersion and the intrusion of newcomers.

Most personal judgments are made from the point of view of a family toward one of its members. Being an ornament or support of the family is more important than just being important in any public sense; which is one reason for the chronic dissatisfaction of creative or ambitious native Philadelphians.

The derivation of family status anywhere is fairly uniform: tenure of power and wealth, a record of distinction somewhere along the line, and connections with other such families of status. In this, Philadelphia is certainly not different from Rome or Kalamazoo. The way to found a family is traditional and is

summed up by that formula attributed to Quakers: "In the first generation thee must do well, in the second marry well, in the third breed well; then the fourth will take care of itself." If Philadelphia has a difference from other centers it is in its emphasis on that marrying second generation. It is not as a rule family founders who are remembered and worshiped, but members of a later generation. What this means is that in Philadelphia inherited position is better than self-made position. Inherited money is better than made money. Where the money came from is something one prefers to forget, no matter how honorable or even exciting the getting of it may have been. A real family just *has* money; and almost the same thing might be said of distinction.

The mere acquisition of wealth may create individual position, but does not make a family. The idea is "wait and

dent of the Bank of the United States and archfoe of Andrew Jackson, who drove him from public life and sent him down in history, quite unfairly, as a symbol of black reaction.

The chairman of this reunion at the Pennsylvania Historical Society was Edward Biddle (1). Others in the group are:

(2) Francis Biddle, Roosevelt's Attorney General; (3) Colonel Anthony J. Drexel Biddle, Marine Corps combat training instructor in World War II and hero of his daughter Cordelia's book My Philadelphia Father; *(4) Anthony J. Drexel Biddle, Jr., United States Ambassador to Poland and Spain.*

see." If a son turns out well, that is, takes the opportunity to become a full-fledged gentleman and marries into an already good family, the chances are that it's a safe bet. His children merely have to consolidate, marry within the same circle, and have lots of properly educated children. Then the family position is fairly secure; somebody along the line is bound to turn up rich and distinguished again to keep things going.

What counts, however, is not the actual wealth or the actual distinction. These are just fine flowers. What counts is the plant itself, the roots, the species, holding on and breeding true through successive generations. There are some pretty acute words in Richard Powell's novel *The Philadelphian:* "Philadelphia society had long ago worked out a procedure for taking in new members. Money and power were important, but

Philadelphia wanted to see if you could produce children and grandchildren who could handle money and power. Marrying well was part of it, but Philadelphia wanted to find out if the blood lines would run true from generation to generation. Proving that you had poise and culture was part of it, but would your children have the same qualities, or would they be freaks and eccentrics: Philadelphia society didn't care for freaks and eccentrics. It had produced very few of them in its two hundred and fifty years of existence. Those few had been removed quietly and quickly, the way a gentleman farmer who was proud of his stock might dispose of a two-headed calf."

No two Philadelphians will ever give you, if pressed, the same answer to a question about which are Philadelphia's first families. It is of course an unseemly question; the particular Philadelphian's

own family is naturally one of them, but modesty compels him to omit his or any other family too obviously related or connected. But certain names are bound to come up, and the two that come up most frequently are Cadwalader and Biddle. The relative standing of the two families in Old Philadelphia's eyes is perhaps reflected in a hoary joke: "When a Biddle gets drunk he thinks he's a Cadwalader." But the best known of all Philadelphia stories concerns the supposed remark of the Prince of Wales, later Edward VII, after a visit to the city: "I met a very large and interesting family named Scrapple and discovered a rather delicious native food called biddle." Old Philadelphians insist that the Biddles are *not* the first family, but if jokes are the index of family standing, as they seem to be in the case of Boston's Lowells and Cabots, then surely the Biddles are near the top.

In Art: A Long Tradition and One True Genius

"Philadelphia," wrote George Biddle in his autobiography, "has its own breed of integrity. It believes in itself, although there is nothing much any longer worth believing in. It respects its own standards, although these standards are inconceivably shallow and antedate in great measure the birth of our nation. It has the logic and the courage to love what it likes, and to mistrust or to dislike anything worth achieving—anything as a rule that is not Philadelphian."

Biddle spoke for a long line of artists who found the city stifling to talent. Yet it certainly has a long and honorable, if curious, aesthetic history; as long and honorable as any town of its age in the world; curious in that only one creative artist, Eakins, is generally acknowledged, in America at least, to be first-rate. Yet many others, Philadelphia-born or Philadelphia-trained or of Philadelphia families or living there, have achieved some renown. The innumerable Peales, Sully, Neagle, Eakins, Anshutz, Beaux, Borie, Watkins, Wyeth, and Stuempfig form an unbroken chain of talent at home; West, Leslie, Sargent, Cassatt, Pennell, the Ash Canners, Biddle, and Sheeler another tradition in exile. Philadelphia can claim some part of all of them, and all of some of them.

The persistence of this artistic tradition is the direct result of the oligarchy's somewhat condescending patronage of the Muses. It was a world of letters, painting, and music supported, created, and maintained largely by Old Philadelphians, with vital help from the German and Jewish bourgeoisie, that made it possible for artists to exist in Philadelphia at all. Painting is the art which has flourished best and longest there. The great tradition begins with the two very different contemporaries Benjamin West (1732–1820) and Charles Willson Peale (1741–1827). Between them they symbolize pretty neatly the two poles, the double bias of Philadelphian, and indeed

American, culture—one the essentially colonial tradition looking to Europe for values and approval, even to the extent of expatriation, the other the native tradition, firmly rooted in Philadelphia itself. These two viewpoints culminate in John Singer Sargent and Thomas Eakins.

Peale, who stayed at home, was one of those crotchety, curious-minded, many-faceted individualists that Philadelphia seems to have nursed so willingly in its great days and so grudgingly later on. The great hobby and profession of his vigorous old age was his museum, containing portraits of Revolutionary heroes

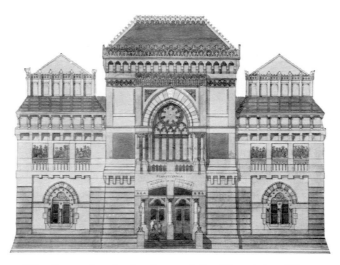

The Pennsylvania Academy of the Fine Arts still occupies the building pictured in this 1876 rendering.

and stuffed animals, for which he rented the second floor of Independence Hall. His greatest coup was the excavation and assembly of the skeleton of two prehistoric mastodons. At eighty-one he painted a fine full-length picture of himself lifting a curtain to disclose the wonders of his museum, mastodons and all.

The Philadelphia tradition of cool, clear, realistic painting, extending through Sully and Neagle, reached its peak in Thomas Eakins. Eakins was a Philadelphian of the intellectual, professional upper middle class; he was much too serious for the Philadelphia upper classes of his time. Brought up on Thomas Sully, Old Philadelphians were quite unwilling not to be flattered. Indeed Eakins's people are not pretty; not half

as pretty as people really are, especially upper-class Philadelphians. A gentleman in Chestnut Hill had Eakins do himself and his wife. He didn't like the results. When the pictures were finished, he sent his check; the pictures were taken to Chestnut Hill; the butler met them at the door, and carted them to the furnace. This was in general the Philadelphia upper-class comment on an artist who violated the appearances.

Eakins taught for ten years at the Pennsylvania Academy, completely reforming and revitalizing the course of study. When in the interests of accurate anatomy he insisted on removing the loincloth from a nude male model posing for a class of women, Philadelphia was finally outraged. Daughters of directors of the Academy were in the class, and those directors saw to it that Eakins resigned.

He lived and died where he grew up, in a substantial house on Mt. Vernon Street, north of Market and thus *déclassé*. The house still stands, though now in a slum, and bears no marker to show that Philadelphia's greatest artist worked there.

For such an old, rich, large city, with so much education and so many advantages and such a long prosperity, Philadelphia may not have lived up to its expectations as a cultural center. Certainly it let slip or snubbed many talents that it might have helped and cherished. On the other hand, as a quite new provincial city in a quite new continent only a metropolis in the last hundred years, without royal or state patronage, founded and influenced by a religious sect that positively hated art, Philadelphia has been an aesthetic miracle. How do Marseilles and Lyon, Birmingham and Glasgow really compare? After a thousand years of culture, has Vienna produced a painter of as much force and weight as Eakins? We are not remembered, as nations or cities, by our talents, who are many, but by our geniuses, who are extraordinarily few.

Charles Willson Peale, founding father of Philadelphia's artistic tradition, painted this picture of himself at the entrance to his museum

Eakins's painting of The Gross Clinic *is a tribute to Philadelphia's great medical tradition. The scene is the amphitheatre of Jefferson Medical College, and the central figure is Dr. Samuel Gross. The great surgeon is explaining a thighbone operation to his students while the patient's mother covers her eyes. Modern viewers may be surprised by the formal clothes worn by Dr. Gross and the other doctors, but what shocked Philadelphia was the realistic depiction of the blood on the surgeon's hands. The painting was refused by the Fine Arts exhibit of the 1876 Centennial and was hung instead in the medical section.*

Eakins's interest in sports, like his interest in medicine, was a faithful reflection of Philadelphia's interest. In the picture above he shows Max Schmitt, his boyhood friend, rowing on the Schuylkill River. Eakins himself can be seen in the further scull. With the possible exception of Winslow Homer, no American artist of his time has brought such authenticity and understanding to the painting of outdoor life.

The picture below of The Fairman Rogers Four-In-Hand *was painted on commission of the coach's owner. Mr. and Mrs. Rogers are seated on the box-seat, with friends on the roof-seat behind them and two grooms on the rumble. For an Eakins it is brilliantly colored, but the horsy set would have preferred the elegance and dash of Sargent. Eakins was too solidly middle-class to quite please Old Philadelphia.*

Philadelphia's leading painter today is probably Walter Stuempfig, who is known especially for his pictures of Manayunk, a factory town on the Schuylkill. The painting at right shows his gift for turning a rather dismal industrial scene into a landscape of charm and romantic beauty.

How Spite Cost Philadelphia Two Great Art Collections

The social exclusiveness of Old Philadelphia has cost the city two out of its three great private art collections. Only that of the lawyer John G. Johnson ended up in the Museum. Those of Joseph E. Widener, the Traction King, and Dr. Albert C. Barnes, the lord of Argyrol, landed elsewhere out of spite.

Widener had made the proper second-generation move of taking an impeccably social wife, the beautiful Ella Pancoast. But this was not enough to win him admission to the Assembly, the annual ball that defines who is in and who is out of Philadelphia society. By the curious double standard of the Assembly, a man who marries outside society may bring his wife into the charmed domain, but a girl who marries "beneath her" forfeits her own membership. (As a young Clothier was told when he sought permission to bring Grace Kelly to a ball: "You'll have to marry her first.") The

Joseph E. Widener   *Dr. Albert C. Barnes*

new Mrs. Widener was dropped. In 1919 their daughter Fifi had one of the grandest of Philadelphia debuts; everybody went, but Fifi nonetheless was one of the debutantes not asked to the Assembly that year. Father Joseph was furious. He tried the kind of blackmail possible in such circumstances; he refused to serve on a civic committee where his presence, and above all his money, was essential—unless Fifi got her invitation. Since the Wideners had now moved from their impossible address on North Broad Street to a pillared château called "Lynnewood

Hall" outside the city (see page 8), the legal minds of the Assembly's Board of Managers found the solution. Fifi was asked as an "out-of-town" guest, still without her mother. Widener was not appeased. He gave his art collection to the National Gallery in Washington.

The Barnes collection is still right in Philadelphia, or at least in Merion, one of the closer Main Line suburbs. But though you can see the Johnson collection in Philadelphia and the Widener in Washington, you can't see the Barnes collection, not easily at any rate, and not if you're an Old Philadelphian; for of all Philadelphia's snubbed parvenus, Dr. Barnes reacted most violently. As a boy who spent much of his bitter childhood among the shacks and dumps of the Neck in southernmost Philadelphia, he seemed to have developed a very special combination of brilliance and truculence.

After making a fortune from a gargle

Philadelphia has always had a "court por-
trait painter," and the present holder of
that unofficial title is Franklin Watkins.
This is his portrait of R. Sturgis Ingersoll,
president of the Philadelphia Museum and
member of the city's most distinguished le-
gal family. He is shown sitting in Watkins's
studio, leafing through an art magazine.

called Argyrol, Barnes moved to the Main Line and took up fox hunting, as a member of the Rose Tree. He was conspicuous for his falls. His courage may have been admired, but his style and manners were not. Though there is no record of his having actual trouble with the other members of the Rose Tree, one can well imagine how definitely he was not included.

He gave up hunting and turned to art, becoming one of the earliest and shrewdest collectors of modern French paintings. In 1923 a Paris exhibition of his Soutines, Modiglianis, and other painters then little known, made an international sensation. Dr. Barnes could hardly wait to share the excitement with Philadelphia. But Philadelphia was not ready for modern art and when the Barnes show opened at the staid Academy, the local critics frothed at the mouth. Words like "unmentionable,"

"infectious scourge," "unclean things," flapped about, and a group of psychologists declared in a public manifesto that "the artists who painted such things were either crazy or moral degenerates." Barnes was rabid with fury, as though he had created the works himself. He wrote ferocious personal letters to the critics, suggesting to a female one that she would never be a real critic until she had relations with the ice man, this being typical of the Barnes approach to an enemy. He couldn't do much to the critics except insult them; but he, like Widener, had his revenge, and it took him the rest of his life.

A Barnes Foundation was created, and a marble gallery built in Merion. Nearly everybody wanted to see the pictures, and almost nobody could get in. The stories of people who tried and failed are as numberless as the stories of people who tried and failed to get into the Assemblies,

the difference being that anybody who danced at the Assemblies was sure *not* to get into the Barnes Collection. Anybody connected with the Academy or the Museum would be, if possible, forcibly kicked out. Insulting letters to the officials of the Museum, Fiske Kimball and Sturgis Ingersoll, press releases and letters to the editor, all just carefully nonlibelous, an attempt to sabotage the WPA art project in Philadelphia because those who ran it had Museum connections, battles with the University's school of Fine Arts—all kept the struggle going. Dr. Barnes drove through a stop sign and was killed in 1951, but the Foundation carries on his fight with Philadelphia. Lawsuits have opened the Barnes museum a crack, but only a crack. The doctor's magnificent collection of Cézannes, Renoirs, and the other great masters of French art remains the most hidden thing in the Hidden City.

Philadelphia's Finest Ceremony: The Insurance Dinner

Insurance in Philadelphia and America began where so many other things began: with Benjamin Franklin. His company was called, and is still called, the Philadelphia Contributionship for Insurance of Houses from Loss by Fire. In order to indicate which houses were insured by the company, it placed on each front wall, according to established English custom, a small lead plaque, bearing a device of four cross-clasped hands. Hence its nickname, the Hand-in-Hand.

The Contributionship gave and gives insurance only on brick and stone buildings in Philadelphia and adjacent counties. The insurance is perpetual. One pays down a lump sum covering risks on a certified building, and after a while dividends are paid back. These limitations, combined with a policy of great caution and selectiveness, have kept the Hand-in-Hand solvent but small.

In 1836 the company erected a large, red-brick, neo-classic building that looks like a modestly pretentious private house. Here the directors' dinners are still held, complete with wines and champagnes, hams supplied as always by Todd in Richmond, terrapin from Cape May, cigars from the old family firm of Wagner. At a table furnished with monogrammed linen, engraved silver, and special china the directors feast about once a month through the winter. The menu for December 18, 1867, lists oysters, two soups, fish, chops, turtle, coquille, ham, chicken and oyster pie, sweetbreads, croquettes, duck, grouse, partridge, terrapin, and omelette.

By the 1880's the company appeared to be interested only in avoiding risks, maintaining assets, and giving dinners. Theatres were not insured—on moral grounds. No investments that paid more than 6 per cent were tolerated. High buildings were considered unsafe, and Philadelphia's first skyscraper, the Bul-

litt building of 1887, was turned down. In general the Hand-in-Hand was said to be interested only in fire insurance on "pig iron below high-water mark."

In 1894 this somnolent state of affairs was rudely shattered by an attempt on the part of rather less Old Philadelphian policyholders to upset the directorship and make the company "progressive." The attitude of the board, they declared, was "that of a mouse snugly ensconced in a rich old cheese." The attempt was quashed. Old Philadelphia stockholders left their deathbeds to vote their confidence in the old order and its taste in Madeiras. When the smoke of battle cleared, the Old Guard was entrenched more firmly than ever.

One would think that even in Philadelphia one such insurance company would be enough. But no; there are two. The second, equally barnacled and Old Philadelphian, is the Mutual Assurance Company for Insuring Houses from Loss by Fire, which was started in 1784 as a protest against the Contributionship. At the time the Contributionship rejected any building that had a tree next to it. Too risky. Then as now, in Penn's "greene Country Towne," trees had their allies. Among them was Dr. Benjamin Rush. He and his tree-loving friends were furious about the Hand-in-Hand's arbitrary rule. Trees were not that much of a risk. Fires usually started inside houses, not outside, especially if the houses were protected by Dr. Franklin's lightning rod. In protest, the tree lovers formed their own insurance company. Just like the Contributionship, it had its own marker which, appropriately enough, bore the device of a bushy tree.

The dinners of the Mutual, or "Green Tree," are, if anything, even more special than those of the Contributionship. After sherry with soup, wine with the fish or meat, champagne with dessert, the ta-

ble is cleared. Each guest then gets a big finger bowl (really a "glass washer," or monteith), with two sherry glasses in it, turned upside down. Around the table, always clockwise, are passed port and Madeira. The two glasses are filled. The chairman raps on the table and calls out, "Gentlemen, are you charged?" The glasses being filled, and the gentlemen thus "charged," the first toast—"To the Mutual Assurance Company"—is drunk. After a suitable pause comes the second toast, "To Washington"—a tradition since 1799 when a messenger interrupted a Mutual dinner with the news of the General's death. If one wanted to pick a single ceremony as the perfect flowering of Old Philadelphia, a good insurance dinner would be it.

Each chair in the dining room has on its back a copper plate on which is inscribed the succession of managers for each managerial post. The succession tends to be pretty much hereditary, or at least family. Biddles have abounded on both boards; one such succession in the Contributionship seems to have consisted of almost nothing but Morrises. At present all the members of both boards, with one exception, are also members of the Philadelphia Club. All the members, except one, are Episcopalians. It goes without saying that all are graduates of Princeton, Pennsylvania, Harvard, or Yale, in about that order.

A man may get to be president of another big insurance company or a bank, may make the Philadelphia Club, may be in Who's Who and the Social Register and loaded with honorary degrees, but the final Philadelphia accolade remains his election to the board of one of these commercially fairly negligible insurance companies. There are very few places higher than this, certainly in the business world at least, to which a Philadelphian can aspire.

and-in-Hand plaques and an old fire hat make a setting for Morris Duane, a director of the Contributionship and descendant of Franklin

The Renaissance of Penn's City

In 1956, on the east side of Washington Square in the old section of the city known as Society Hill, Richardson Dilworth, who was then mayor of Philadelphia, built a town house. No such house had been built anywhere in Philadelphia since 1930, and very few since 1900. Indeed, the town house for the past thirty years had been pretty much of an anachronism. Of the some eight thousand listings in the Philadelphia Social Register, less than three hundred give "center city" addresses. "Nobody lives in town," is the local cliché.

Nevertheless, firmly at the back of the Old Philadelphian's mind is the atavistic memory of the family town house. Such a house, if established before the twentieth century in some proper location, is in fact a sort of necessary patent of gentility. To have had no genuine town house or to have had a genuine town house in the wrong place, such as North of Market, remains forever a sort of bar sinister on the family escutcheon. Old Philadelphia gossip is full of not very nice stories about North-of-Marketers who first moved to the suburbs to cover their tracks, then sneaked back to Rittenhouse Square hoping nobody would notice.

For more than a century, however, the social tide has been running out of the city to the suburbs. Wealthy citizens from the time of Penn had considered themselves country gentlemen, but it took the Railroad to start the great exodus of Old Philadelphia to the new towns on the Main Line. The evacuation begun by train was completed by automobile. The 1920's saw the almost complete removal of upper- and middle-class Philadelphia from the city to the suburbs.

The effects were disastrous. The wholesale decay and destruction of old houses and the consequent blight on city real-estate values were outward signs of inward corruption. The owners of the city abdicated. Removed beyond the range of city taxes and city politics, they lost all interest in city reform. Since they didn't have to see what was happening, they didn't care; Philadelphia became another demonstration of the dangers of absentee landlordship. And Philadelphia achieved another of its firsts: the first American city to be destroyed by its transportation; first the railroad, then the local transit system of trolleys, and last the automobile, which in turn began to destroy the railroads and the transit system and is now destroying the suburbs themselves.

Deserted by its national leaders, ruled by Republican political bosses like the crude (though Old Philadelphian) Boies Penrose, the city won the scornful description "Corrupt and Contented." So it remained until the 1950's when a reform movement, backed by Old Philadelphian business leaders as well as such New Philadelphians as John B. Kelly and Albert Greenfield, captured City Hall. Its leaders were Joseph C. Clark and Richardson Dilworth, both Democrats but both Old Philadelphians, Clark by birth, Dilworth by adoption.

The clean sweep of political reform has had a striking influence on the physical renovation of the city. The National Park Service had already begun work in the historic district around Independence Hall, clearing away most of the buildings, preserving a few monuments like Biddle's and Girard's neo-classic banks, and filling the space between with a whole series of charming brick-walled gardens. Then with the coming of the reform administration, the City Planning Commission produced a scheme for the renovation of a whole area of the city, south to Lombard Street, west to 7th Street, in what is loosely called Society Hill. This plan is now actually being put into effect. It is one of the most daring and most tasteful pieces of town planning in the world, an attempt to salvage what is good of the old and what is needed of the new, and in general to transform that part of the city into a sort of urban residential paradise without making a museum fossil out of it.

This revival in the older part of the city is the single most attractive and exciting part of the Philadelphia Renaissance, and has most vitally intrigued Old Philadelphians. Remodeling old houses is, after all, one of Old Philadelphia's favorite indoor sports, and to be able to remodel and consciously serve the cause of civic revival all at once has gone to the heads of the upper classes like champagne. Following the example of Mayor Dilworth in his move to Washington Square, family after family has returned to its city roots.

The Planning Commission has much more grandiose projects, and has already executed some of them, including the new Penn Center on the site of the old Broad Street station and its "Chinese Wall" of railroad tracks. Acres of the most hideous slums in the world have been torn down and in their places have been erected decent and sometimes even nice-looking modern row houses or low apartments or even skyscrapers, surrounded by lawns and trees and walkways and playgrounds. There is in fact a vast redoing of the city that is quite outside the orbit of most Old Philadelphians.

If the bad habits of years don't overtake the city again, Philadelphia may someday find herself, if never again the capital or first city of the country, at least the only American city really fit to live and work in, the only city where educated taste and the requirements of ordinary human beings are considered along with commercial razzle-dazzle and real-estate values, the only city where tradition is respected but not allowed to destroy imaginative experiment, and where, in sum, Penn and Franklin might return to feel at least spiritually at home.

From the tower of City Hall, in the foreground, a bronze William Penn surveys his changing city. This is the opposite view from that on pages 6–7, with the Museum at upper right and the Schuylkill in the background. To the left of City Hall tower is Penn Center, a key project in Philadelphia's current downtown redevelopment plan.

In W. P. Frith's painting of 1844, Mary Stuart weeps at Knox's harsh retort to her, while John Erskine kneels and tries to comfort her with "m

By H. R. TREVOR-ROPER

THE QUEEN WEPT, THE PREACHER STOOD HIS GROUND

Two great figures dominate the history of Reformation Scotland. Far above the anarchy and barbarism of those impersonal, overmighty noblemen who divided the power of the Crown, we can still see the clash of two real, vivid personalities. On one side is Mary Stuart, the beautiful, unfortunate, romantic queen who sought to set up a Renaissance court, perhaps a Renaissance despotism, in that impossible country; on the other stands John Knox, the unyielding Old Testament prophet who, out of the same anarchy, sought to build a new, revolutionary, Puritan society. For six crowded years Mary reigned in Scotland, before being driven first from her throne, then from the country, by her exasperated subjects. For most of those years Knox was a minister in Edinburgh. And on five occasions they met, face to face. It was the meeting of Jezebel and Elijah; and the most vivid chronicle is by Elijah himself: Knox's own great *History of the Reformation in Scotland,* written in the very style of the Book of Kings.

How can one do justice to the drama of those famous encounters? The contrast is complete: a contrast of personalities, of ideas, of whole worlds. Mary Stuart was one of the great Renaissance women, like Isabella d'Este or Lucrezia Borgia or Queen Elizabeth. Born in Scotland a few days before her father died, she had been brought up a Frenchwoman in the court of France. Her mother's family, the family of Guise, was itself a princely house, rulers in Lorraine, the most magnificent, most brilliant, most ambitious family in France. It dominated the French crown and was an independent power in Europe. Mary Stuart, in her youth, had been taught politics, and had learned conspiracy, under her uncles the Duke and the Cardinal of Guise. Her mother, Mary of Lorraine, a masterful, dauntless woman, had been Regent of Scotland. She herself had been, though briefly, Queen of France. She had been taught poetry by Ronsard; she sang and danced and played the lute; she devoured romances of chivalry—devoured them so successfully that her own life became one.

But Mary was not a court princess only. Her natural gaiety always broke through. Her "dear sister" of England, Queen Elizabeth, maintained a hieratic magnificence, made solemn "progresses" through her obedient country, and is commemorated by the number of starched, bejeweled dresses she wore and heavy four-poster beds in which she slept. Mary was an altogether wilder figure. Her strong passions, of love and revenge, led her into desperate actions. If she loved gentle poets and musicians—the Frenchman Chastelard and the Italian Rizzio, both of whom paid with their lives—she yielded finally to the ruffian Bothwell. She regretted that she was not a man "to know what life it was to lie all night in the fields, or to walk upon the causeway with a jack and knapsack, a Glasgow buckler, and a broadsword." In her hectic life she was often in undress or in disguise—she would flee from her subjects "in man's clothes, booted and spurred," be recaptured by them in an undersized red petticoat, escape again disguised as a servant: her knowledge of the country was acquired not in stately progresses but in wild rides. When her lover Bothwell was ill at Hermitage Castle, she would ride twenty-five miles over the moors to see him,

...sing words of her beauty"

and back the same day; when Rizzio had been murdered before her eyes in Holyrood House, she would gallop for two hours by moonlight to Dunbar, seeking revenge; escaping from her eleven-month captivity in the island-fortress of Lochleven, she would ride all through the night, and cross the Firth of Forth to reach Hamilton. Her last escape was the most dramatic of all: for ninety-two miles over moor and forest she would never alight from her horse; for two nights she would sleep on the ground; she would feed only on oatmeal and buttermilk; and at last, in an open fishing boat, she would cross the Solway into England and another nineteen years of ever-changing confinement and incessant conspiracy, ending on the block.

Finally, to complete the portrait, there is her irresistible charm, which softened the strongest Protestant: "I think there be some enchantment," wrote one of them, "whereby men are bewitched." Mary bewitched the stony-hearted nobility of Scotland into overlooking her religion and her crimes; she bewitched the conspirators who sought to murder Queen Elizabeth and place her on the English throne; and she has bewitched historians ever since, bewitched some of them into believing even the strongest evidence against her to be forgery.

One man, however, she never bewitched. Long before he had met her, John Knox had made up his mind. To him the whole world of the Renaissance, that florid magnificence sustained by an unequal society, was odious. Its culture was a pagan culture, its Church a pagan church, rooted in injustice; and nowhere was the injustice greater than in Scotland, to whose long-neglected poverty this borrowed Italian splendor was a vulgar mockery. Fleeing from Catholic Scotland to Protestant England, and from the re-Catholicized England of Mary Tudor to Calvinist Geneva, Knox had found there at once his master and his model. Calvin's city was, to him, "the most perfect school of Christ since the time of the apostles," and having seen it, the future of both England and Scotland was clear to him. To prepare the way he issued from Geneva his challenge to the feminine sovereigns of both countries, *The First Blast of the Trumpet against the Monstrous Regiment of Women.*

It was an unfortunate publication. In that very year, 1558, Mary Tudor died, and her sister Elizabeth became at once the Protestant queen of England and the savior of the Gospel in Scotland. Returning to take advantage of the change, Knox sought to explain himself to the new queen, but his explanation was neither gracious nor complete. He would admit that Elizabeth was an exception, but he bluntly maintained the general rule: the monstrosity of feminine government. He had to maintain it, for already another popish queen was reaching for her sceptre. Only a year after Knox's return to Scotland, Mary Stuart's mother and husband both died, and she set out, as queen regnant of Scotland and queen pretendant of England, to mount in Edinburgh an assault on the Protestantism of Scotland and England alike.

So the stage was set. The scene was Scotland, but the struggle was not only a Scottish struggle: against that grim, remote background a European contest was to be fought out. First France, then Spain would be behind Mary: she could and did raise revolution against Elizabeth in England, just as Elizabeth could and did raise it against her in Scotland. She was not a good Catholic, either in faith or morals. She would murder her second husband and marry her third with Calvinist rites. The Pope, the King of Spain, the Queen Mother of France, all regarded her with horror. And yet, as they said, it was through that door or none that Catholicism could be restored in England and Scotland: the House of Guise was the hope of the Counter Reformation, and Mary was its essential instrument. And on the other side, Knox was hardly less cosmopolitan. His ideas had been formed in Geneva, his style in England. He, too, was the agent of an international system. In France, in the Netherlands, in the Rhineland—wherever it was weak—the old society found itself challenged by the new; the pagan Babylon by the Christian Jerusalem. Scotland was but one small, distant theatre of this great struggle. But it was a key theatre, and the struggle there was exceptionally dramatic because there, thanks to the overshadowing nobility, Princess and Prophet faced each other on almost equal terms.

The first personal encounter was in September, 1561. Knox had thundered in the pulpit against the idolatry of the Mass and was summoned before the Queen for raising sedition both by his sermons and by his famous *Blast of the Trumpet*. In his defense he minced no words. It was not sedition, he said, but his plain duty to expose and rebuke "the deceit, pride and tyranny of that Roman Antichrist," and his trumpet-blast had not been directed against Mary Stuart but against "that wicked Jezebel of England." So long as Mary did not defile her hands with the blood of God's saints, he would be as content to live under her "as Paul was to live under Nero." But he would keep his own religion, not hers: Did not the Jews keep theirs under their infidel rulers, Pharaoh and Nebuchadnezzar? "Yes," replied Mary, swallowing the unflattering comparison, "but none of those men raised the sword against their princess." That, replied Knox, was simply because God had not given them the power. "Well, then," said the Queen, slowly recovering from the spate of words, "I perceive that my subjects shall obey you, and not me; and shall do what they list, and not what I command: and so must I be subject to them, and not they to me." Not at all, replied Knox, so long as she followed not her own will but reason— reason which distinguished "the immaculate spouse of Jesus Christ" from "the Roman harlot . . . altogether polluted with all kind of spiritual fornications." The Queen could not make this distinction, and Knox drew the logical conclusion. "If there be not in her a proud mind, a crafty wit, and an indurate heart against God and His truth," he said afterward, "my judgment faileth me."

year later there was a second encounter. Knox had heard that the Queen "had danced excessively, till after midnight," no doubt to celebrate the persecution of the Huguenots in France, where "her uncles were beginning to stir their tails, and to trouble the whole realm." So he preached against her and was duly summoned to explain himself. He did so, and forcefully, comparing himself with Christ denounced to that "proud Herod" who had exchanged the head of John the Baptist for "the dancing of a harlot's daughter." The Queen replied mildly that she would not argue about her uncles, "but if ye hear anything of myself that mislikes you, come to myself and tell me, and I shall hear you." "Madam," replied Knox, "I am assured that your uncles are enemies to God and unto His Son Jesus Christ; and that for maintenance of their own pomp and worldly glory they spare not to spill the blood of many innocents"; therefore God would take His revenge of them. But as for Mary, he would not tell her her sins in private: "I am called, Madam, to a public function within the Kirk of God, and am appointed by God to rebuke the sins and vices of all." If she wanted to hear him on the subject of her own sins, she had better come to his public sermons.

The next year there was an outbreak of persecution against the Catholics of Scotland and Mary again sent for Knox. Did he allow, she asked, that her subjects should thus take the sword of justice into their own hands? Knox did indeed allow it. He reminded her of the prophet Samuel who "feared not to slay Agag, the fat and delicate king of Amalek, whom King Saul had saved"; of "Jezebel's false prophets, and Baal's priests," rightly slaughtered by Elijah; and of Phinehas who, though no magistrate, "feared not to strike Cozbi and Zimri in the very act of filthy fornication." Whereupon the Queen, "somewhat offended, passed to her supper."

A month later came the most famous encounter of all. The Queen was preparing to marry her second husband, Lord Darnley, a Protestant who, however, brought her the support of the English Catholics. Knox at once moved to the attack. In the Cathedral of St. Giles, in Darnley's presence, he delivered a long, fierce sermon against this "infidel marriage," reminding Darnley of the punishment of Ahab "because he would not take order with that harlot Jezebel." At this, Darnley rose and left the Church; even Protestants were outraged; and Knox, summoned immediately to Holyrood, found the Queen "in a vehement fume," crying out "that never Prince was handled as she was."

"'I have,' said she, 'borne with you in all your rigorous manner of speaking, both against myself and against my uncles; yea, I have sought your favors by all possible means. I offered unto you presence and audience whensoever it pleased you to admonish me; and yet I cannot be quit of you. I avow to God, I shall be once revenged.' And with these words scarcely could Marnock, her secret chamber-boy, get napkins to hold her eyes dry for the tears; and the howling, besides womanly weeping, stayed her speech." So runs the preacher's own account.

When an opportunity came, Knox replied. All the Queen had to do, he said, was to give up her errors; then she would find in his free speech "nothing offensive." Even as it was, he only let himself go in the pulpit, "and there, Madam, I am not master of myself, but must obey Him who commands me to speak plain, and to flatter no flesh upon the face of the earth."

"But what have ye to do," interposed the Queen, "with my marriage? Or what are ye within this Commonwealth?"

"A subject born within the same," he replied; "and albeit I neither be Earl, Lord, nor Baron within it, yet has God made me (how abject that ever I be in your eyes) a profitable member within the same." So he went on to denounce the marriage, and once again "howling was heard, and tears might be seen in greater abundance than the matter required." John Erskine of Dun sought to soothe the Queen with flattery, "but all that was to cast oil in the flaming fire." Nor would Knox relent: he must speak the truth and "sustain (albeit unwillingly) your Majesty's tears rather than I dare hurt my conscience, or betray my Commonwealth through my silence."

So that was that. It was clear that Mary would get nowhere with Knox. Even her tears, which served her so well with others, were powerless with him. At their next encounter she twice reproached him with having reduced her to tears, but he stood firm and, once again, compared her with Nero. Thereafter they met no more. After the murder of Rizzio the local cold war became hot and Edinburgh could no longer hold both at the same time. Only when Mary was in prison in Lochleven Castle did Knox return to demand her execution. At the same time, writing his *History*, he turned suddenly aside from his text to denounce "that whore in her whoredom," and hoped God would inspire "a multitude to take the same vengeance upon her that has been taken of Jezebel and Athaliah . . . for greater abomination was never in the nature of any woman than is in her, whereof we have seen only the buds; but we will after taste the ripe fruit of her impiety, if God cut not her days short."

Five years later came the crunch. In France, with the Massacre of St. Bartholomew, the House of Guise seized power, once again, over the Crown. In one of his last sermons Knox denounced that infamous action which seemed to presage the ruin of Protestant Europe. But this time Queen Elizabeth was prompt. Early the next year her army entered Scotland, besieged and captured Edinburgh Castle, and ruined the last hopes of Mary. For another fifteen years Mary herself remained the center of Catholic, Spanish conspiracy; but not now against Scotland. In Scotland the battle was over. Mary was in exile, Knox in his grave; but history had decided between them. In those five famous encounters, Knox had won.

This essay by Dr. Trevor-Roper, Regius Professor of Modern History at Oxford, is one of a continuing series on historic confrontations.

By LINCOLN BARNETT

WHO IS BEHIND THE ASSAULT ON ENGLISH ?

The Bible and Webster are mutilated, the new poets must be decoded, correct speech itself is "undemocratic." The ad men debase the language consciously, and admit it; but do the "look-say" teachers, the government jargon-makers, and the pedants of social science know the harm they do?

"When I use a word," Humpty Dumpty said, in a rather scornful tone, "it means just what I choose it to mean, neither more nor less."

"The question is," said Alice, "whether you can make words mean so many different things."

"The question is," said Humpty Dumpty, "which is to be master—that's all." Lewis Carroll, Through the Looking-Glass

In this playful dialogue Lewis Carroll prophetically defined an issue that a century later would involve teachers, writers, lexicographers, linguisticians, and plain lovers of the English language in a bitter and protracted conflict. Warfare came into the open in the autumn of 1961 with the appearance of *Webster's Third New International Dictionary.* But for several decades, beginning before World War II, hostilities had simmered along in academic communities and in journals of literary and social comment.

In a casual view the battle could be seen merely as a continuation of the unending debate between grammarians and anti-grammarians, purists and "progressives," conservatives who cherish tradition and form in language and free-talkers who believe that linguistic evolution should not be impeded by the past. There have always been protectors of the native tongue in every civilized land, ranging themselves against the forces of vulgarity and verbicide. Their current alarm over the despoiling of English speech may appear to differ only in intensity from that of other generations. But there is a new note. For today they find themselves arrayed not only against the perennial legions of illiteracy (centered in the electronic citadels of the Age of Noise), but engaged also in another quarter by a far more formidable host conscripted from those who have been, supposedly, custodians of the English language in America.

Rather unobtrusively, so far as the lay public is concerned, the teaching of English in schools and the training of English teachers have become increasingly dominated by the discipline known variously as Structural Linguistics, Descriptive Linguistics, or Modern Linguistic Science. Its precepts, which grew out of studies of North American Indian tongues, sound innocuous: (1) language changes constantly; (2) change is normal; (3) spoken language is *the* language; (4) correctness rests upon usage; (5) all usage is relative. But harmless as these ideas seem individually, their total effect in practice has been the annihilation of traditional rules of grammar, the denial of any standards of "right" and "wrong" in speech or writing, and an anarchical philosophy of usage summed up by one of its exponents as: "Any word means whatever its users make it mean." Humpty Dumpty hardly put it more baldly.

Not since the early years of the eighteenth century has such concern been expressed over the decline of literacy and the deterioration of the English tongue. But the reasons for anxiety two centuries ago were notably different from those of today. In the so-called Augustan age of England (c. 1700–1750) reflective men of letters were clamoring for a kind of language authority that did not yet exist. There was no defini-tive English dictionary, and there were no set rules of spelling. As early as 1693 John Dryden, who became poet laureate barely a half-century after Shakespeare's death, had observed that "we have yet no prosodia, not so much as a tolerable dictionary, or a grammar, so that our language is in a manner barbarous." Dryden confessed that he often found it necessary to phrase his thoughts in Latin before he could express them precisely in English. Swift similarly lamented, in 1712, the absence of any fixed standards to which writers might repair. Underlying his desire for a dictionary to stabilize the English language in supposedly permanent form was a conviction he held in common with other writers of the Augustan age. The native tongue, as they could plainly see, was changing at a rate that would render it unintelligible to readers a few generations hence. Even the poet Edmund Waller, writing shortly after the Restoration, had declared:

> *Poets that Lasting Marble seek,*
> *Must carve in Latin or in Greek;*
> *We write in Sand. . . .*

But there was a growing burden of doubt among other men of letters as to the possibility of ever fixing any language in permanent form. For them the historic Anglo-Saxon dislike of regulation applied to every area of human affairs; just as Englishmen never saw fit to frame a written constitution, so they were not prepared to fetter their tongue—which had so splendidly shown its capacity for free flight in the soaring stanzas of the Elizabethan poets—and commit it to a council of academicians.

The state of the language, alas, reflects the state of the culture

Nevertheless, the English language did get a dictionary, compiled by Dr. Samuel Johnson after seven years of solitary and dedicated effort, and published in two folio volumes in 1755. Despite its well-known flaws—its prejudices (e.g., Johnson's famous definition of oats as "a grain, which in England is generally given to horses, but in Scotland supports the people"); its pedantry ("Cough: a convulsion of the lungs, vellicated by some sharp serosity"); and its inclusion of outlandish inkhorn words ("ariolation," "dignotion," "incompossible")—the publication of Johnson's dictionary represented a turning point in the history of the English language.

The other great need of eighteenth-century men of letters was for a grammar, and this was filled in 1761 by that remarkably versatile scientist and philosopher, Joseph Priestley, best known as the discoverer of oxygen. Priestley's excellent pioneering work, *The Rudiments of English Grammar,* not only marked the dawn of interest in English grammar as a subject for scholarly consideration but enunciated vigorously the modern thesis that language is a fluid, ever-changing entity, and hence that general usage must be the arbiter of speech. Within the next two years three other grammars appeared, and in 1776 George Campbell published his influential *Philosophy of Rhetoric,* dealing with questions of taste and style.

In formulating their rules, the eighteenth-century grammarians relied to a large extent on the precedents of Latin and Greek. But to this traditional view a counterpoint began to emerge. In his *Philosophy of Rhetoric* Campbell declared: "It is not the business of grammar . . . to give law to the fashions which regulate our speech. . . . The grammarian's only business is to note, collect, and methodize them." From this premise Campbell went on to define the concept of *usage,* to which he and Priestley accorded final authority, as "present, national, and reputable use." By "reputable use" Campbell meant, "whatever modes of speech are authorized as good by the writings of a great number, if not the majority of celebrated authors." Campbell's definition of "usage" was the accepted one on both sides of the Atlantic throughout the nineteenth century and indeed until a very short time ago.

Differences between American and British usage have appeared mostly in the realm of vocabulary and pronunciation—the spoken word. The literary language has remained more or less uniform throughout the English-speaking world. And Noah Webster helped to make it so. In 1789 he wrote: "The two points therefore which I conceive to be the basis of a standard in speaking, are these: *universal undisputed practice,* and the *principle of analogy* [in its eighteenth-century context "analogy" meant reason, logic, or consistency]. *Universal practice* is generally, perhaps always, a rule of propriety; and in disputed points, where people differ in opinion and practice, *analogy* should always decide the controversy." Supported by these precepts, and sustained by a national consensus of the educated and those who aspired to education, the American language evolved in an orderly fashion—sweeping words into its lexicon from all the varied stores of its polyglot clientele, striking off new coinage, transmuting dusty meanings into bright ones, wielding its resources with daring and gusto—but still preserving its links with the past.

What, then, has interrupted this ordered evolutionary process? What has plunged the American language into a state of chaos? Sounds of alarm rang from coast to coast upon publication of the third edition of *Webster's New International Dictionary.* The nation's critics saw in the philosophical stance of Webster III a betrayal of trust, an abdication of responsibility for the treasure of our tongue, and a surrender to all the flabby, flaccid forces of permissiveness, formlessness, and mindlessness that have fogbound the arts, paralyzed education, and nurtured what the late James Thurber called "our oral culture of pure babble." To some observers it held ominous connotations for the future. For the state of the language reflects the state of the culture, and the decay of language is both symptom and cause of the decay of institutions.

This is the era of the Spoken Word. But is it worth listening to?

Ever since the invention of the vacuum tube, the cocked ear has increasingly supplanted the perusing eye as the main sensory receptor of the American people. This may justify the third tenet of Structural Linguistics, "spoken language is *the* language," and its application in the compiling of Webster III (though I suspect that whenever anyone consults a huge unabridged dictionary, ninety-nine times out of a hundred it is to check either on a written word or one that is about to be written). There is no denying, however, that we live in the epoch of the Spoken Word; and the discovery of the transistor, for which three Bell Telephone physicists won the Nobel Prize in 1956, has now made it possible for anyone to get the Word—electronically amplified and packaged in a plastic case no bigger than a book—wherever he may be. The question is, What does it say?

Quite possibly it may say, "Let us help you to accessorize your kitchen," or "Eat peanut brittle, like when you were little." But one must not confuse the medium with its content. By extending the range of the Spoken Word over barriers of space and time, electronics has nurtured man's indolent proclivity for talking rather than writing. The Spoken Word comes naturally, but it requires both discipline and a set purpose to induce a normal healthy American to sit alone in an office and reduce a welter of blubbery thought to lean and sinewy prose. For writing starts and ends with thinking, and thinking is work for which the primate musculature and sympathetic nervous system were never made. It is much easier to put through a long distance call, dictate long and loosely to a tape recorder, attend a conference or committee meeting, down Martinis at a company lunch or creative cocktail hour, and bustle around the clock from appointment to appointment in a ritual that affords a sensation of activity if not of work.

Any look at the state of literacy in the United States should no doubt begin with the largest single category of reading matter: the comic book. It is perhaps not generally known that the total annual circulation of comic books is greater than the combined annual circulations of the nation's twenty largest mass magazines. The comic books struck their bonanza during World War II when they became the almost unchallenged reading staple of America's armed forces (on land, on sea, and in the air), among whom magazines like *Life* and *Look* were regarded generally as highbrow publications. To this day the comics have retained their hold on the juvenile reading audience, a category ranging from preschool levels to middle age.

It goes without saying that all exponents of traditional disciplines in education—*i.e.*, hard work and intellectual substance—would happily see all comic books burned. On the other hand, it should surprise no one familiar with our pedagogical establishment that many educational theorists and child psychologists defend comic books on the grounds that (1) it is better for the children to read comics than nothing at all; (2) a child who begins by reading comic books sometimes develops a taste for the printed word and goes on to tackle real books; and (3) bloodshed, violence, and gore in the so-called "horror" comics sublimate the child's subconscious aggressions—better for him to enjoy mayhem in his "imaginings" today than commit the real thing in junior high. (This venerable postulate has in recent years been adopted and reiterated with renewed vigor by those who profit from sex and slaughter on television.)

"The language of mutilation," or how Madison Avenue consciously corrupts English

So far as the language of comic books is concerned, it must be said that the authors of many of the "quality" comics (those endorsed by various educational organizations or *Parents' Magazine*) restrict themselves scrupulously to standard usage. But countless others, whether "animal" or "horror" types, are shot through with sound effects—POW! WHAM! BONG!—denoting impact, as well as the drab spectrum of phatic monosyllables—*Huh? Duh. Blaa! Whee! Yikes! Ug! Glub! Wha?*—with which much of teen-age America informs the world of its state of being.

For all their enormous circulation—some 600 million a year —comic books probably exert no more influence on the use of English in this country than do the editorials of the New York *Daily News,* America's biggest newspaper, on political thought. Quite apart from other factors (such as their violence and general inanity), I am inclined to suspect that the quality of dialogue found in most of the comics is considerably superior to that used by their readers. So one must look elsewhere for the source of infection. As Jacques Barzun has observed: "The ignorance of the unlettered takes no scrutiny to establish. What we need to plumb is the ignorance of the educated and the anti-intellectualism of the intellectual."

In purely quantitative terms of verbal output—words, words,

words—the most profuse source and proliferous disseminator is the great sprawling complex of advertising. And here we do indeed find a corrupting influence on the national tongue and one, moreover, that is consciously designed and ingeniously employed to corrupt. That usually amiable essayist, E. B. White, wrote caustically of Madison Avenue jargon not long ago: "With its deliberate infractions of grammatical rules and its crossbreeding of the parts of speech, it profoundly influences the tongues and pens of children and adults . . . it is the language of mutilation."

The English Department at Princeton University maintains a bulletin board to which it regularly affixes choice specimens labeled variously "No-English," "Doublespeak," "Minitrue," and the like. Some recent cullings: *Contact-less Lenses— comfort-contoured to your cornea curvature . . . Ready-to-eat Protein for ready-to-eat People . . . White Sale—Bamberger's brings you a riot of pretty colors . . . Try Ripple Wine—in two delicious flavors—red and white.*

The significant fact about Madison Avenue's linguistic abuses and misuses is that they are not the slapdash errors of unlettered hacks, but the carefully conceived creations of educated writers and editors. Their grammatical distortions are conscious devices, gimmicks to catch attention—like the patch over the eye of the shirt model, or Commander Whitehead's beard, or the tattoo on the hand of the Marlboro smoker. It is a credo of the "advertising psychologists" retained by all the big agencies that colloquialisms and vulgar usages establish a rapport with the mass audience.

From time to time advertisers are summoned before Congressional committees to justify their language. In a recent inquiry spokesmen for certain food packagers were asked to explain their use of such expressions as "jumbo" and "full quart" (as opposed to "quart") and in particular the classification of olives and prunes as "giant," "colossal," and "mammoth" rather than "small," "medium," and "large." One witness, a "motivational research expert" for the olive and prune packers, provided an answer rich with the idiom of his expertise. "Our entire social structure," he proclaimed, "depends on the mass production of psychologically satisfying products as much as the individual depends on these products in fulfilling his emotional needs." Words like "colossal" and "mammoth" are "more meaningful" than "large" or even "very large," he said, adding that "customers do not want small prunes at any price."

The constant, conscious corrosion of the English language by the Madison Avenue semanticists was sharply criticized at the centennial of the University of Michigan Law School in 1959 in an address by Ralph M. Carson of the New York bar. "What we have in advertising," he said, "goes beyond the device admired by Talleyrand of using language to conceal thought; the *beau idéal* of all motivational selling is the use of language to conceal the *absence* of thought."

Another great abattoir of language is politics, as it has ever been throughout history. Somewhat more than twenty-three centuries ago the resumption of peaceful relations between

Athens and Sparta after the Peloponnesian War was frustrated by the inability of the warring Greeks to understand each other after three decades of hostilities. "The meaning of words had no longer the same relation to things," the historian Thucydides related, "but was changed by men as they thought proper." In our own epoch the deformation of meaning for dialectical ends has been so common a practice, especially in totalitarian states, that any cautious reader or auditor of the news automatically takes pains to select the proper referent when he encounters terms like "democracy," "freedom," "justice," "patriotism," "law," "people," "progressive," "reactionary," and the like. And the disease spreads continually, affecting new concepts, new countries. Just recently a Western diplomat in Africa complained to an American reporter, "The Communists have expropriated all the good words —anti-colonialism, African personality, Pan-Africanism. How are we supposed to beat that?"

Verbicide (as the murder of a word was termed by C. S. Lewis) is only one of many methods by which politics mounts an assault on language. In addition to their small-scale guerrilla operations against individual words, politicians and their accessories, the bureaucrats, wage a kind of slow-poison warfare against the whole corpus of the language by stuffing it full of indigestible, fatty, polysyllabic verbiage. Although defenders of literary style in England complain of the Officialese dispensed from Whitehall,* the British product seldom compares with the suety offerings exuded from our political steam tables in Washington, as well as from the various state capitals and municipal council chambers throughout the nation. "The grossest thing in our gross national product today is our language," James Reston, chief Washington correspondent of the New York *Times* wrote recently. "It is suffering from inflation."

"The torrent of unintelligibility," or how Officialese and Academese stultify meaning

Reston's criticism applied to the language in both its spoken and written forms. For samples of the former, one need look no farther than the transcripts of any of the new-style Washington press conferences (dating from 1952) in which touchy questions, formerly quashed with a curt and presumably undemocratic "No comment," are now met squarely with a torrent of unintelligibility. (The strategy, of course, was not invented in 1952. As Oscar Wilde once wrote, "Nowadays to be intelligible is to be found out.") The written variety of Officialese is equally distended, but usually for another purpose: the wish of the author to magnify or escalate (favorite new

word in Washington) the importance of a trivial utterance by grandiloquent terminology.

No less stupefying than this form of verbal dropsy is another, quite different malady of Officialese induced apparently by some notion of conserving language through the use of abbreviations and acronyms. The practice began during the New Deal with the advent of NRA, AAA, FCC, NLRB, SEC, WPA, and the other so-called alphabetical agencies. They continued to proliferate in ensuing years—most exuberantly, perhaps, in the mazes of the Pentagon. Today most newspaper readers can translate SAC and NORAD, and perhaps even DEW Line (Distant Early Warning Line), SAGE (Semi-Automatic Ground Environment), and BMEWS (Ballistic Missile Early Warning System). But probably few outside the armed forces are aware that FAGTRANS stands for "first available government transportation" or that SODTICIOAP means "special ordnance depot tool identification, classification, inventory, and obsolescence analysis program." The richest elixir of Pentagonese, however, is to be savored in that arcane language which the military employ purely to communicate with one another. The following is a recent order issued to members of an infantry unit at Fort Jackson, N.C., announcing their transfer to Fort Dix, N.J. and thence overseas: "161 Fol EM Pvt (E-2) unoindc PMOS TOS ETS BPED PROFILE ind rel asg Trne Org Indc USATC INF (3161) this sta rsg US Army OS Repl Sta (1268) Ft Dix NJ for mvmt to USAREUR charged to Jul Aloc for ultimate rsg OS units indc Pers WB immu IAW AR 40-526 immed upon rec of this order . . ." and so on for another dozen lines.

The deadening influence that official jargon can exert upon thought was a topic that preoccupied the late George Orwell. In his novel *1984* he recounted dramatically how a government in total control of all media of communication can and will so degrade language that words are drained of meaning, the process of thinking becomes impossible, and there is no truth save what those in power define. He developed the same thesis further in an essay, *Politics and the English Language,* shortly before he died. Citing the downward spiral of the alcoholic who drinks because he feels himself a failure and then fails more dismally still because he drinks, Orwell observes: "It is rather the same thing that is happening to the English language. It becomes ugly and inaccurate because our thoughts are foolish, but the slovenliness of our language makes it easier for us to have foolish thoughts. . . . The great enemy of clear language is insincerity. When there is a gap between one's real and one's declared aims, one turns as it were instinctively to long words and exhausted idioms, like a cuttlefish squirting out ink. . . . But if thought corrupts language, language can also corrupt thought."

Officialese, or the jargon of government, however, flows limpid as a mountain stream beside the jargon of pedantry, or Academese. Where the author of Officialese wishes most of all to sound important, the author of Academese is usually a specialist in some rather restricted field that he regards as his

---

* In *The Reader Over Your Shoulder* the British authors Robert Graves and Alan Hodge characterize "Whitehallese" thus: "The official style is at once humble, polite, curt, and disagreeable; it derives partly from that used in Byzantine times by the eunuch slave-secretariat, writing stiffly in the name of His Sacred Majesty."

private preserve. Cherishing his exclusivity, he affects a language bristling with esoteric terminology and barricaded against comprehension by the amateur. Actually, little talent is required to write jargon; it demands neither grace nor clarity, and these are the most difficult qualities for a writer to achieve.

A few years ago I assisted in compiling the findings produced by one of those portentous projects on "The National Purpose" into which the big foundations like to put their money from time to time. My work involved collating mountains of papers, treatises, and transcripts of symposia and distilling them into summaries of reasonable size. The task was arduous, and I was distressed after some weeks to discover that my reports were being rewritten—at far greater length—by the editor in charge, a professor of political science at Harvard. He explained, when I questioned him, that my reports had been too compressed, had "packed too much material into too little space." I replied that I had always considered a ratio of maximum content to minimum space an objective of good writing. He said, "Well, my impression is that you've been straining for lucidity."

For an actual example of full-blown Academese one need only turn to any of the learned journals that luxuriate in the rich gardens of educational theory—and open to any page. The specimen that follows is taken from a recent issue of the official magazine of the American Educational Research Association, Washington, D.C., and picked (quite at random) from the opening section of an article entitled *Meaningful Learning and Retention: Intrapersonal Cognitive Variables:* "Much more saliently than in experimental laboratory types of learning situations, typical school learning requires the incorporation of new concepts and information into an established cognitive framework with particular organizational properties. The transfer paradigm still applies here, and transfer still refers to the impact of prior experience upon current learning. But prior experience in this case is conceptualized as a cumulatively acquired, hierarchically organized, and established body. . . ." etc., etc.

Of Teachers College,
"in-basket factors," and the
jargon of social "science"

The headwaters of the great turbid stream of Academese lie somewhere back in the caves of nineteenth-century German scholarship, where no philosopher was worthy of the name unless he evolved his own System, Method, and Lexicon. But a major tributary now flows along the frontiers of modern science. To interpret events within the atom, as well as those in the outer universe, physicists have had to resort to increasingly abstract ideas and increasingly complex mathematical techniques. Observing the prestige of natural science, the social scientists have aspired to loftier status, too. Today books and papers in every branch of the social sciences are not only adorned with strange and occult terminology but riddled with mathematical symbols, and crosshatched and hemstitched with probability tables, sine curves, and other picturesque fashions in charts and graphs. As an example of the new quantitative mode in social science, I cite a paper entitled *In-Basket Tests and Factors in Administrative Performance*, based on a study conducted in 1960 under a grant to Teachers College from the U.S. Office of Education. The problem was to evaluate 232 school principals from all over the United States on the basis of their responses, over a period of five days, to a flow of materials—memos, queries, complaints—that were fed into the in-basket on their desks. Each was presented with the same material: "memo pads, letterheads, paper, pencils and paper clips. . . . He was not to say what he *would* do—he was to *do* it. He actually wrote memos, called meetings, prepared agendas." It was in the analysis and correlation of these in-basket performances that the real mathematical fun began:

The 120 x 120 matrix was factored. An orthogonal factor matrix composed of the first ten factors was rotated to form an oblique matrix having a factor structure as nearly as possible like that found for the original in-basket factor analysis. Coefficients were computed which reflect the relative relationship of each of the 120 variables to each of eight oblique reference vectors, each vector corresponding to one of the eight in-basket factors..

The paper wound up with the conclusion that "a powerful technique" had been found for judging school administrators.

A distinguished scholar, bothered by the buzz of Academese about him, has remarked dourly that in the world of education today, "Communication occurs by good luck." For it is not only in science and social science that jargon prevails. Its accents dominate the discourse of the arts and humanities, the language of literary, aesthetic, and musical criticism. One need not explore every compartment of criticism, for the same curtains of cumulo-nimbus rhetoric enshroud them all. I submit as an archetype of the modern critical mode this brief review of an exhibition by a young American painter which appeared in a recent issue of *Art News:* "Since many of these forms are discontinuous, her themes of concentricity and incrementation are carried by striping or surfing their edges to make archipelagoes which lift and sway like cobras across the often burnished surface, as in *Three Towards Four*, with its gleaming gold Rapunzel ambiance and diffident organic calligraphy. But these larger pictures are transitional. More certain, solid, and (as usual) beautiful are the smaller works, with their earth-gem colors and cycloid, gyring, oculomotility and explicitness of generative warmth. . . . There is something very American about the intense inner plasticity of her reach and vision."

The fundamental principles of critical jargon are (1) avoidance of the explicit and (2) concealment of the absence of thought by means of pretentious, technical, impenetrable verbiage. Thus in the passage cited above, the reader must hack his way through such thickets as "diffident organic calligraphy" and "intense inner plasticity of reach and vision." These are garlands of Academese in purest form. But elsewhere in the passage there are phrases in a different but still distinctly contemporary American style. I refer to "archipelagoes which lift and sway like cobras" and "gleaming gold Rapunzel ambiance." These have the timbre of Pure Creative Writing.

Of poetry, "free-write," and not getting "hung up" on grammar—or meaning

If one is searching for springs of language undefiled by pedantry, politics, or motivational vector analysis, what more likely place to look than the domain of belles-lettres? For is it not reasonable to assume that poets and novelists—craftsmen who employ the English language for aesthetic ends—must cherish its form and harmonies, respect its structure and traditions, and employ its rich, orchestral resources with veneration and care? But somehow a funny thing happened to creative writers on their way to 1963. In poetry two tendencies appeared. One derives from T. S. Eliot, whose erudition and use of symbolism, multiple imagery, and masked illusions—as manifested most strikingly in *The Waste Land*—engendered what has been termed the Footnote, or Cryptographic, school of poetry; this has to be decoded rather than read. Its offerings are characterized, as a rule, by scrupulous adherence to the classical disciplines of meter and rhyme on the one hand, and on the other by utter inscrutability.

The second main current in modern poetry flows in the opposite direction. Here the objective is to cast off the restraints of traditional poetic forms and sing with unpremeditated ecstasy. The evolution of free verse from Whitman down through Sandburg and the poets of the twenties and thirties is a familiar chapter of literary history and only relevant here because of what happened to it at the hands of the beatniks. For along with the ad writers and pedants, the beatniks are enemies of the language. They have no organized speech. For the most part they are determinedly anti-verbal, communicating by grunts, grimaces, and interjections. Their use of "man" and "like" may be somewhat equivalent to the average person's occasional "er," a species of stammer. However, a perceptive observation on the beatnik's use of "like" has been made by Walker Gibson, poet and Professor of English at New York University, in a recent essay: "The beats, in their crude and sloppy way, of course, have surrounded much of their language with a metaphorical blur by using . . . the simple device of 'like.' They suggest, with this blur, their conviction of the im-

possibility of anybody else's doing any better with words. Only squares believe you can speak 'precisely.' "

The prototype, of course, is Jack Kerouac's *On the Road*, and a passage in the first chapter of that book not only illustrates the style but provides an insight into the beatnik writer's *modus operandi:*

As far as my work was concerned he said, "Go ahead, everything you do is great." He watched over my shoulder as I wrote stories, yelling, "Yes! That's right! Wow! Man!" and "Phew!" and wiped his face with his handkerchief. "Man, wow, there's so many things to do, so many things to write! How to even *begin* to get it all down and without modified restraints and all hung-up on like literary inhibitions and grammatical fears."

I personally have never had the experience of writing with an audience, even of one, hanging over my shoulder and yelling "Wow" or "Phew" (or even "Boo!") as the little black letters appeared on the big white page. The testimony of most writers suggests that the act of writing is generally a solitary effort for which applause, if any, is long deferred. It is not, I think, one of the performing arts.

Quite apart from the watcher by the writing machine, the phrases "literary inhibitions" and "grammatical fears" are revealing. For in their crude way they epitomize the thinking of one school of writing (and of teachers of composition) today. The underlying premise is that the aspirant writer, the future poet or novelist, must express himself freely; that his talent will atrophy if he gets "hung up" on rules of grammar and syntax. This notion derives from a wedding of modern educational theories (of which more later) with the literary precedent of James Joyce. Endowed with neither the erudition or poetic genius of Joyce, exponents of the "free-write" school have found in his works (if they ever read them) chiefly the demise of sentence structure and a sanction for unintelligibility. One would think that in *Finnegans Wake* Joyce had extended his genre to its ultimate limits. But no. We have today a new technique of "writing" that is analogous to the collage in the field of painting, photography, and the cinema. William Burroughs, whose novels have been praised by many critics—most notably by the astute and acidulous Mary McCarthy—described it in a recent issue of *The Transatlantic Review:*

Pages of text are cut and rearranged to form new combinations of word and image — In writing my last two novels, Nova Express and The Ticket That Exploded, i [sic] have used an extension of the cut up method i call "the fold in method" — A page of text – my own or some one elses – is folded down the middle and placed on another page — The composite text is then read across half one text and half the other — The fold in method extends to writing the flash back used in films, enabling the writer to move backwards and forwards on his time track — For example i take page one and fold it into page one hundred — I insert the resulting composite as page ten — When the reader reads page ten he is flashing forwards in time to page one hundred and back in time to page one —

He then provides a specimen of the technique, a fold-in of lecture notes, texts from several writers, and newspaper articles. Here is one fragment:

On reflection we can discover cross references scrawled by some boy with scars — The last invisible shadow caught and the future fumbles for transitory progress in the arts — Flutes of Ali in the door of panic leaves not a wrack of that God of whom i was a part — The future fumbles in dogs of unfamiliar dust — Hurry up — Page summons composite mutterings flashing forward in your moments i could describe — The deja vue boatman smiles with such memory orders —

What does one find in this progress from the early experiments of Joyce and Gertrude Stein in the 1920's to the fold-in collage of the 1960's? First, it is evident that what began as an attempt to achieve new fluencies of expression and mood by renouncing certain traditional forms and disciplines has culminated in the abandonment of all form, all discipline—and all meaning. But words do nothing at all if they are emptied of meaning. Language is wholly cerebral: it is an artificial medium of communication. It was devised by man, it is unique to man, and it works only when men agree on what its components mean.

The Bible turns to the idiom of Rotary, and Webster's to Polly Adler

The war against the English language is thus a many-pronged offensive, waged amid jungles of jargon, over oceans of Officialese, prairies of pedantry, mountains of meringue, while the air oscillates with electronic frenzy. The common bond that unites the foe is utter disdain for the reader. Each saboteur at the typewriter keyboard is preoccupied solely with his own objectives. Whether for reasons of indifference, incapacity, or indolence, he chooses to ignore Dr. Johnson's crucial precept: "What is written without effort is in general read without pleasure." Writers of the past respected this axiom and sometimes rephrased it in other ways, as did Yeats, for example, who wrote:

A line will take us hours maybe,
Yet if it does not seem a moment's thought,
Our stitching and unstitching has been naught.

Anatole France expressed it thus: *"Caressez longtemps votre phrase, elle finira par sourire."* And in the final chapter of *The Elements of Style* (which he revised and expanded from the original work by William Strunk, Jr.), E. B. White observes, "Writing is, for most, laborious and slow. The mind travels faster than the pen; consequently, writing becomes a question of learning to make occasional wing shots, bringing down the bird of thought as it flashes by." (White himself is the best shot in the country today.)

Signs of disintegration of the language might have gone un-noticed by the public for several years—despite skirmishing, infiltration, and the fall of isolated redoubts—had it not been for the collapse of two major bastions of the mother tongue: the Bible and the Dictionary. Early in 1961 the New Testament section of the New English Bible appeared,* latest in a long line of revisions of the King James Version (its most recent predecessor being the Revised Standard Version of 1952). Since the King James Version and the works of Shakespeare have generally been ranked together as the noblest monuments of the English language, many laymen wondered why the majestic seventeenth-century translation could not be left alone. For in all Christendom it is only the English Bible that is regarded as a great work of literature. The intent of the translators of the new version was twofold: to correct textual errors in the King James Version revealed by recent discoveries of new manuscripts and, by rendering it in "frankly contemporary English" (changing *thou* and *thee* to *you*, for example), to make it as "readable" as any other book. Unfortunately a good many readers have felt that although the objectives of scholarship may have been fulfilled, the new version has simply stripped away the beauty and splendor of the old without any notable addition to understanding. Even such an upholder of the contemporary idiom as Bergen Evans (who has staunchly defended Webster III against its critics) confessed to being disturbed by its style. Remarking that most of the changes seemed to him "unnecessary and even harmful . . . mere busy-work," Evans wrote in the New York *Times* magazine: "In achieving the blandness of contemporary expository prose, the inoffensive language of a commercial civilization, the translators have been dismayingly successful. . . . Maybe the Bible can't really be translated into contemporary prose. The poetic archaism of the King James Version—with its majesty, its stupendous music, its moving eloquence, its wildness and passion—may be ideally suited to its subject. Can Ecclesiastes, for instance, really be stated in the idiom of Rotary? Does the Book of Job lend itself to the language of *The Reader's Digest* or Isaiah to the speech of the tabloids?" On the other side of the Atlantic Ocean, T. S. Eliot dismissed the new version as "a combination of the vulgar, the trivial, and the pedantic."

The reaction to the New English Bible seemed but a murmur, however, in comparison to the explosion touched off by the publication a few months later of *Webster's Third New International Dictionary*. In brief, the editors of Webster III were charged with abrogating their responsibility as custodians of the language by: (1) blurring to the point of obliteration the traditional criteria for distinguishing levels of usage—e.g., they had dropped completely such warning labels as "colloquial," "erroneous," "illiterate," and employed the terms "non-standard" and "slang" with a caution amounting to reluctance; (2) including hundreds of transitory and dubious expressions as standard; (3) expunging a quarter of a million words from the literary past, with the cut-off date arbitrarily set at 1755; (4) discarding illustrative citations from the classics in favor of contemporary utterances by, among others, Bob Hope, Billy

* See "The Bible Is Given New Speech" by Gilbert Highet in HORIZON for March, 1961.

Rose, Jimmy Durante, Art Linkletter, Ethel Merman, Polly Adler, and Willie Mays; (5) compounding misunderstanding by refusing to discriminate clearly between words often confused (such as "semimonthly" and "bimonthly," "depreciate" and "deprecate"). And indeed, the Editor in Chief, Dr. Philip B. Gove, did not repudiate the charges. On the contrary, he made it clear that in his view verbal usage is simply a matter of social usage, an aspect of etiquette. A dictionary, he declared, "should have no traffic with . . . artificial notions of correctness or superiority. It must be descriptive, not prescriptive."

Dr. Gove's viewpoint—and his dictionary—have had their defenders as well as their detractors. Arrayed overwhelmingly, almost unanimously, against Webster III were professional writers, journalists, critics, professors of literature and the humanities, and lovers of the language in general. On the other hand, it was approved by educational theorists, many English teachers, and all apostles and exponents of Structural Linguistics (of which Dr. Gove is one). As the adversaries clashed violently, in print and on the air, the public became dimly aware of certain developments that faculty members in liberal arts colleges and universities and other observers of trends in education have known for a long time—namely, that the teaching of English has undergone a revolution in the past three decades and that this revolution has, as Dwight Macdonald wrote in *The New Yorker*, "meshed gears with a trend toward permissiveness, in the name of democracy, that is debasing our language by rendering it less precise and thus less effective as literature and less effective as communication."

Taught on "look-say" methods, Johnny can't read and College John can't write

For some years before the issues burst into the open, however, businessmen, lawyers, editors, personnel managers of corporations, and deans of admission had been complaining that today's college graduates (to say nothing of high-school graduates) cannot spell, punctuate, or organize their thoughts in coherent verbal form. From various quarters some disquieting communiqués made their way into public view. For example:

• A report entitled *The National Interest and the Teaching of English*, published by the National Council of Teachers of English in 1961, disclosed that some four million U.S. school children have "reading disabilities," that approximately 150,000 students failed college entrance examinations in English in 1960, and that 70 per cent of American colleges and universities find it necessary to offer remedial work in English.

• The University of Pittsburgh recently tested 450,000 high

school students and found that only one out of one hundred could produce a five-minute theme without errors in English.

• An English examination at New Jersey's Fairleigh Dickinson University disclosed that less than one quarter of the freshman class could spell "professor" correctly.

• Dean William C. Warren of the Columbia University School of Law declared in his annual report for 1955: "We have found that few of our entering students, however carefully selected, possess these skills [reading and writing] to the extent needed for law study."

• Dean Erwin N. Griswold of the Harvard Law School reported in the same year that numbers of applicants to his school, otherwise apparently acceptable, offered college records showing no courses in literature or language (or, for that matter, in mathematics, science, or philosophy), but consisting wholly of such subjects as Principles of Advertising Media, Office Management, Principles of Retailing, Stage, and Costume Design, and Methods in Minor Sports.

• Dean Jacques Barzun of Columbia recently asked a class of 170 first-year graduate students in history to explain the meaning of twenty common abbreviations—B.C., A.D., e.g., i.e., *ibid.*, and the like—plus one date in Roman numerals. Of the 170, only one understood all twenty abbreviations, only seventeen understood more than fifteen, about half the class understood no more than four, and of that half not one could translate MDCLIX into 1659.

• An official of the National Broadcasting Company declared in 1962: "Recently we interviewed over one hundred college graduates to fill a post calling for a knowledge of good English. Not one of them made the grade. None of them knew the rules of good writing, and none of them could express himself in clear, simple, forthright English sentences."

What produced this sorry state of affairs? In its 1961 report the National Council of Teachers of English confessed, with some understatement, "Neither informed laymen nor leading teachers of English are satisfied with the results of present-day English teaching." To the extent of 140 pages (complete with charts and tables), the authors of the report set forth their analysis of the problem. First and foremost, they declared, many English teachers are inadequately educated for their calling, and many state departments of education don't seem to care. They documented the argument with some revealing facts:

• Approximately half of all high-school English teachers never completed a college major in English.

• Nineteen states certify elementary-school teachers without any specified requirement in English.

• Twenty-one states certify elementary-school teachers without any requirements in reading or "children's literature."

• Only half a dozen states have English specialists in their departments of education, though virtually all states have specialists in home economics and driver education.

• Only 41 per cent of the colleges that prepare high-school English teachers require a course in advanced composition, only 39 per cent require a course in grammar and usage, only 33 per cent require work in world literature, and only 20 per cent require study of contemporary literature or literary criticism.

Having presented these illuminating statistics, the report then hit out in all directions, finding such reasons for the shortcomings in the teaching of English today as crowded classrooms, overloaded schedules, and inadequate library facilities (doubtless legitimate complaints), poorly planned buildings, lack of co-ordination among states in the absence of national standards, lack of proper supervision, lack of articulation in English curricula from grade to grade, lack of tape recorders, record players, and other mechanical aids, and lack of "basic pedagogical research and experimental planning."

The report also included some recommendations: "If the teaching of English is to be improved throughout the United States, bold and direct action must be undertaken nationally." This would involve "large-scale programs supported by Congressional appropriations or massive co-ordinated programs sponsored by independent educational foundations." And what would these large-scale, massive co-ordinated programs consist of? Well, among other things: "Special study of the problems of articulation in all institutes and all conferences. . . . Establishment of regional centers for study and demonstration of sequential, articulated programs in English. . . . Development of regional centers for preparing and distributing sample teaching aids. . . . Assistance to architects and administrators in planning ideal facilities for English instruction. . . . Experimentation in using electronic, audio-visual, and other aids to improve English teaching."

As one caustic advocate of old-fashioned teaching methods observed after studying this report, "It seems to have been written from the moon." * For, as might be expected, it uttered not a single word about the factors that almost everyone outside the cloisters of pedagogy (including an increasingly voluble number of parents) holds responsible for the prevalence of student illiteracy today. To many it seems obvious that the reasons Johnny can't read and College John can't write inhere not in any need for sequential, articulated programs or audio-visual aids, but in the theories and practices of American education as they have luxuriated in the past thirty years.

John Dewey has taken much of the blame for the deterioration of educational rigor, the emphasis on adjustment rather than achievement, the supplanting of competition by conformity, and the substitution of discussion for study. Actually, Dewey never denigrated the disciplines of the mind. It was his apostles and exegetes, proliferating in the mushroom cellars of Columbia's Teachers College and thence disseminating the spores of pedagogic theory across the land, who diverted the course of education away from the pursuit of knowledge and toward the cloudy goal of "preparation for life."

The bill of particulars against modern pedagogy is a lengthy one and has been fully presented elsewhere. But as to the teaching of English and the promotion of literacy in particular, the most violent storms center around the "whole-word," or "look-say," method of reading instruction, the contrivance known as

* Of an earlier report by the same organization Jacques Barzun once declared, "The volume is one long demonstration of the authors' unfitness to tell anybody anything about English."

"vocabulary control," the prevalence of fatuous readers and reading lists, and the universal employment of multiple-choice, or punch-card, examinations.

Under the "look-say" reading system, a pupil is taught to recognize words as homogeneous units instead of building them up through knowledge of the alphabet and syllabification. Although the traditional phonic system, which was standard until the educational revolution of the thirties, is returning to some schools, others do not expect a child to know what a syllable is until the third grade or to know the order of the alphabet until junior high. According to a recent study by the Council for Basic Education, a child taught by the "look-say" method generally commands a vocabulary of some 1,300 words by the end of the third grade, while a child taught by the phonic method has a vocabulary twice that size by the end of the first grade. As a matter of fact, the great Italian educator Maria Montessori showed more than half a century ago that children learn to read best by learning to write—by translating familiar sounds into visual symbols, rather than the reverse. But Montessori is long forgotten, and in modern education writing is considered a secondary and even peripheral skill.

"Vocabulary control," or why Russian first-graders read Tolstoy and ours "A Funny Sled"

Equally controversial and, it would seem, even less defensible, is the strange device known as "vocabulary control," which is expressly designed to hold down the number of words a child may learn at any given time. Under the assumption that gulping too many new words at a sitting may give the tender young reader a case of verbal indigestion, textbooks are confined within rigidly restricted word lists which are let out an inch or so at a time from grade to grade. Thus in the fourth grade the U.S. school child uses a primer of some 1,800 words. The Russian child, according to a recent comparison of American and Soviet school systems, has a primer of 2,000 words in the first grade and of 10,000 words in the fourth. He is, moreover, reading Tolstoy in the first grade while Johnny is working his way through books entitled *A Good Big Fire, The Blue and Yellow Boats,* and *A Funny Sled.*

Within the limitations of "vocabulary control" and "word frequency lists," the primers are bound to be dull; and as the grades roll by the texts used in English classes continue to be delimited by various restrictions. It is not only the ever-present fear of controversy, of sex, or of the American Legion and other book censors that holds down the range of permissible reading matter. The educationists have imposed a variety of controls of their own, born of the sensational discovery that knowledge of literature is useful not for its own sake, but because of the "positive values" it may impart. In his informative book *The Schools* Martin Mayer quotes a member of the English Department at Teachers College who proclaimed authoritatively: "You can teach the same values with Edna Ferber as you can with Shakespeare." And indeed Edna Ferber ranks high on many a secondary-school reading list.

Another institution hostile to literacy is the multiple-choice examination, for it demands of the student only an X on a dotted line rather than the sustained intellectual effort of marshaling his thoughts and expressing them coherently in an ordered structure of language. The reasons for its inception and universal use are well understood: there just aren't enough examiners to grade millions of essay-type questions, and computing machines are faster and cheaper. Nevertheless many thoughtful educators look upon them with concern. For one thing, the phrasing of the questions is often imprecise and ambiguous, and a bright student who can discern several possible answers to a question is more likely to select a wrong answer than another who has less imagination. The case against the multiple-choice, or "objective," test has been best epitomized by Dr. Banesh Hoffmann, Professor of Mathematics at Queens College. Their basic defect, he says, is that "they call for choices but not reasons for choices. . . . Defective test questions tend to turn multiple-choice tests into lotteries. . . . For multiple-choice tests, by their very nature, tend to favor the pickers of choices over the doers, and the superficially brilliant over the creatively profound. And the use of these tests has a baleful influence on teachers and teaching."

How grammar, that is, rules, lost out to "Structural Linguistics," that is, no rules

Far more baleful, however, than any of the other circumstances contributing to the demise of literacy and the degeneration of English has been the abandonment of grammar in favor of "modern linguistic science." The enmity between upholders of traditional grammar and the exponents of Structural Linguistics runs deeper than any other conflict in the whole battleground of education. And the Structural Linguists appear to be winning. In a single generation they have driven grammar, as it was taught to everyone who is now over forty, out of most of the public schools of the country. They have infiltrated the English departments of many teachers' colleges, influenced the training of student teachers, and thus affected the teaching of English to children in public elementary and secondary schools.

They have, as noted earlier, taken over Webster's Unabridged Dictionary. And they dominate the National Council of Teachers of English, which accounts, of course, for the fact that the Council's melancholy reflections on the sad state of English teaching place the blame on everything but the practice of teaching itself. Its most recent report clearly reflects its bias through the recurring use of such phrases as "traditional eighteenth-century Latinate grammar," "old-fashioned grammatical apparatus," "language superstitions," "substitution of a scientific attitude for eighteenth-century assumptions," and "pressure of the demand for traditional grammar from the uninformed." On the other hand, the report acclaims the "spectacular advances that have been made in the field of descriptive linguistics," adding that "these advances . . . constitute a breakthrough comparable to those in physics and mathematics."

What kind of breakthrough? Since there is only the murkiest understanding of Structural Linguistics outside its own domain, it must be explained that the term involves both a method and a set of principles. The method has proved of enormous worth in several varied fields. It is the essential tool of cultural anthropologists concerned with studies of languages outside the Indo-European family, and especially those of primitive people without a system of writing. It is extremely useful to certain language teachers whose function it is to impart a quick, practical grasp of a second (*i.e.*, foreign to the student) *spoken* tongue. And by virtue of its painstaking techniques of vocal sound analysis, it has greatly assisted communication engineers in the design of equipment for the transmission of speech, data-processing machines, and digital-to-sound transducers.

But the Structural Linguists are not—and have not been for the past quarter-century—content with a role as objective scientists, collectors of data, technicians, and taxonomists. They have a *Weltanschauung* that embraces psychology, sociology, and education, and they propagate it with evangelical fervor. It is, therefore, their "basic principles" that have aroused a conflict which has spread far beyond educational circles to the nation at large. These principles have been stated most succinctly by Dr. Robert A. Hall, Jr., Professor of Linguistics at Cornell University, in his book *Linguistics and Your Language:*

There is no such thing as good and bad (or correct and incorrect, grammatical and ungrammatical, right and wrong) in language.

There is no such thing as "written language." There is speech and there is writing; and of these two, speech is basic in human life and writing is a reflection of speech. Changing the writing is not changing the language.

A dictionary or grammar is not as good an authority for your own speech as the way you yourself speak.

Words do not have any "real" meaning as opposed to other "false" meanings. Any meaning people give to a word is automatically its *real* meaning under those circumstances [*cf.* Humpty Dumpty].

All languages and dialects are of equal merit, each in its own way.

When languages change, they do not "decay" or become "corrupted"; a later stage of a language is worth neither more nor less than an earlier stage.

43

Inasmuch as Structural Linguistics developed in the United States out of the quiet work of a few anthropologists engaged in the study of Athapascan, Algonquian, and other American Indian tongues, it seems astonishing that such a remote and highly specialized realm of scholarship could engender the extraordinary precepts enunciated above or exercise such a powerful effect on standards of English—the most widely used language in the world—and the methods of teaching it in schools.

Linguistics began to evolve from philology in the latter half of the nineteenth century, and the most important events occurred in France and Russia. In Paris a young scholar named Ferdinand de Saussure (1857–1913) conceived the idea that structure, not grammar, was the key to language analysis. In a series of lectures, published only after his death, he showed that language is never a mere sequence of words, like beads on a string; on the contrary, each and every language in the world is a complex structure or system that can be analyzed *without regard to meaning*. For his contribution De Saussure is generally regarded as the founder of modern descriptive linguistics. Of no less importance was the formulation by the Russian linguists Baudouin de Courtenay and Nikolai Kruszewski of a concept that provided the basic tool of linguistic analysis: the unit of speech known as the phoneme. Armed with the phoneme, linguists are able to isolate, analyze, and record the vocal sounds of any language in the world without recourse to alphabets or other existing calligraphic codes. The phoneme has been called the molecule of speech, and like the molecule of chemistry it is not a fundamental or irreducible particle but a rather complex entity with properties about which linguists do not always agree.

From the study of primitive tongues, linguisticians derived a rule: Usage is all that counts

In the United States the great anthropologist Franz Boas of Columbia University made extensive studies between 1897 and 1908 of the languages of various American Indian tribes which, of course, had no script, no history, and had never before attracted scholarly interest. But it was not until the second and third decades of this century that Structural Linguistics came to full flower in the work of two men who are universally recognized as its American progenitors. One was Boas's brilliant student Edward Sapir (1884–1939), who investigated the language and culture of the Wishram and Athapascan Indians of the northern Pacific coast. The other was Leonard Bloomfield (1887–1949) of Chicago, a behaviorist, who first worked intensively on Menominee, a branch of central Algonquian still spoken in Wisconsin and around the Great Lakes, and later made a study of Tagalog, the language of Luzon and now the official tongue of the Philippine Islands.

Their early studies were pursued with enormous patience in the face of enormous difficulties—for the languages they undertook to master had no written script whatever. By the tedious process of questioning native speakers day after day, week after week, they eventually began to discern distinct forms and elements in what had seemed at first an impenetrable vocal blur. Many of the sounds articulated by the Indians could not be represented by the familiar letters of the Roman alphabet. The grammar—a term defined by Bloomfield as "the meaningful arrangements of forms in a language"—was utterly different from that of English, Latin, or any of the Indo-European tongues. But the linguists discovered that the Indian languages shared certain elements not only with each other but with all other languages in the world. In short, they had found—and it was their most important accomplishment—a means of analysis that could be universally applied without reference to the terms and concepts of traditional grammar. From the pioneering work of Sapir and Bloomfield the more detailed methods and principles of Structural Linguistics subsequently evolved. Amid the fog of Academese that now engulfs the subject, a few of its basic ideas and details of methodology can be distinguished.

To begin with, the Structural Linguists, as noted earlier, concern themselves only with the spoken language. The low esteem in which they hold writing derives in part from the statistic that only about 5 per cent of the world's four thousand languages have any written form. "Language," as defined by an official publication of the Linguistic Society of America, is "a system of arbitrary vocal symbols by means of which a social group co-operates." The three words "arbitrary," "vocal," and "symbol" are all significant. Taking them in reverse, words are *symbols* because they are not identical with the objects and events they denote; they have meaning, but they must not be confused with their referents. They are *vocal* because they are produced by the human voice, as opposed to other auditory symbols (sirens, bells, Morse code), visual symbols (pictures, gestures, writing), and tactile symbols (Braille). A written word, therefore, is merely a visual symbol of a vocal symbol, and both are completely arbitrary. They are arbitrary because "It is convention alone—a kind of tacit agreement among the members of a social group—that gives any word its meaning." There is no reason other than social consensus why a quadruped of the species *Equus caballus* should be called *horse* in English, *cheval* in French, and *Pferd* in German. Even onomatopoetic words (from which, some theorists have suggested, human speech arose) vary from one language to another. Thus a dog goes *bow wow* in English, *wauwau* in German, *bubu* in Italian, *wan wan* in Japanese, and *ouâ-ouâ* in French.

From the premise that the tacit agreement of the social group gives any word its meaning, the Structural Linguists have extracted their axiom that usage is determined solely by vox populi and that if an "error" or "incorrect form" becomes sufficiently prevalent, then it is no longer an error and no longer incorrect, whatever purists may say. Language changes constantly; it ceases to change only when it ceases to be spoken—e.g., classical Greek (Latin continued to change down through the Middle Ages).

Since popular usage is the ultimate and not-to-be-disputed arbiter of language, the Structural Linguist simply describes, he does not prescribe. His *modus operandi* is to observe and study the speech of a particular social group, to ascertain its characteristic patterns, and to define and classify the arrangements and relationships of linguistic forms within the over-all structure. A description of these patterns, arrangements, and relationships constitutes a description of the structure, or grammar, of the language.

An abstruse discipline,
based on Stone Age cultures,
is applied to our language

The primary interest of the linguistician, however, is the sound of a language; and it is in the field of phonetics—or, more specifically, phonemics—that Structural Linguistics has erected its most elaborate methodological edifice. The starting point of linguistic analysis, as noted above, is the phoneme. But the curious fact is that no two Structural Linguists define it in the same way—a fact that has led some captious critics to remark that their contempt of writing doubtless stems from their inability to write. Here are a few of the attempts that have been made, over a quarter of a century, to describe the fundamental tool of the trade.

Leonard Bloomfield in *Language:* "A minimum unit of distinctive sound-feature."

Bernard Bloch and George L. Trager in *Outline of Linguistic Analysis:* "A class of phonetically similar sounds, contrasting and mutually exclusive with all similar classes in the language."

Simeon Potter, Baines Professor of English at the University of Liverpool, in *Language in the Modern World:* "A class or bundle of sounds of phones, no two of which can ever take each other's place in the same environment."

Webster III: "The smallest unit of speech that distinguishes one utterance from another in all of the variations that it displays in the speech of a single person or particular dialect as the result of modifying influences."

The reason for the apparent confusion surrounding these definitions is that the phoneme is both an entity and a composite of lesser entities. Thus the initial sounds of *pit* and *bit* are different phonemes. The initial sounds of *keep, cool,* and *coal,* as well as the final sound of *rock* are all varieties of the phoneme

/k/, although they are physiologically and acoustically different. Such varieties of the same phoneme are called allophones. The possible number of allophones for a given phoneme is far greater than the untrained ear ever discerns.

Once the component phonemes of a language have been distinguished and classified, the next step in linguistic analysis is to discover how the phonemes are built up into morphemes. A morpheme is the smallest unit of lexical meaning—which is not to say that a morpheme is necessarily a *word*. In the terminology of Structural Linguistics a morpheme is defined (by Bloch and Trager) as "any form, whether free or bound, which cannot be divided into smaller meaningful parts." The key terms here are "free" and "bound." Words like *cat, book,* and *home* are examples of single free morphemes. Words like *cats* and *catty, books* and *bookish, homes* and *homely* contain two morphemes, of which the secondary morphemes—*s, ty, ish,* and *ly*—are bound, for they cannot appear alone and have lexical meaning.

The total store of morphemes in any language is its lexicon. A lexicon in itself, however complete, tells little about a language unless it is augmented by understanding of the meaningful arrangements of its component forms. To ascertain how morphemes are arranged in larger patterns, the linguistic analyst must listen attentively for a variety of small and subtle signals. He must cock his ear, for example, to the matter of juncture: the difference between *an aim* and *a name, I scream* and *ice cream, night rate* and *nitrate.* He must discern nuances of stress—as disclosed in the pronunciation of the noun *con·vict* versus the verb *con·vict',* or the phrase *black bird* versus the compound *blackbird.* Some expressions are differentiated by a combination of both stress and juncture—for example, *all together* versus *altogether, lighthouse keeper* versus *light housekeeper.*

More important than these sound signals, however, is the question of *order*—the sequence of elements in a larger form. In English and most other modern Indo-European languages order is all important, for (to lapse into the vocabulary of classical grammar) they have in common the basic sequential pattern of subject-verb-predicate. For example, the description of an event is reversed completely if one says *Man bites dog* instead of *Dog bites man.* Both statements are grammatical, but the meaning depends on the order in which the elements are spoken. Linguisticians are firm, moreover, in their insistence that grammar has nothing to do with meaning—a *grammatical* statement need not be *meaningful* or significant in a semantic sense. Thus Dr. Noam Chomsky of the Massachusetts Institute of Technology, one of the younger stars in the linguistic galaxy, cites two word strings: (1) *Colorless green ideas sleep furiously* and (2) *Furiously sleep ideas green colorless;* and observes that although both series are nonsensical, the former constitutes a perfectly grammatical sentence.

When the order of a language has been discerned, the linguistician can then identify "form-classes," which is to say the components that can fill a functional slot in a given construction. For example, in the sequence *The . . . was good,* the open slot can be filled with certain forms like *concert, food, skiing, liquor*, but not with others like *cerulean, argued,* or *nevertheless.* To the Structural Linguist the term "form-classes" connotes approximately what "parts of speech" means to those educated in the "outmoded concepts of eighteenth-century Latinate grammar." Structural Linguistics divides form-classes into two main headings, *function words* and *content words.* Function words are those which operate largely as a means of expressing the relations of grammatical structure—the so-called "particles," "conjunctions," "prepositions," and "auxiliaries" which constitute the cement and mortar of the house of language. Content words fall into three classes: *things, actions,* and *qualities*—corresponding to "nouns," "verbs," and "adjectives or adverbs." To those who inquire why the old terminology had to be revised, the Structural Linguist replies that the traditional parts of speech were first defined by Greek grammarians, then adopted by the Romans, and subsequently applied to modern Indo-European languages. In English, as everyone who has ever studied traditional grammar knows, there is often great difficulty in distinguishing adverbs from prepositions (like *up* and *before*), and many nouns and verbs are interchangeable (*slice* of ham, *slice* the ham). In languages outside the Indo-European family, moreover, the classical terminology often does not work at all: their sentences do not follow the subject-verb-predicate pattern, and their lexicons contain many words that cannot be classified in the Greco-Latin framework. In the Hopi language, for instance, events of brief duration—*lightning, wave, flame, meteor, puff of smoke*—have the character of verbs, although *cloud* and *storm*—concepts of longer duration—resemble nouns. Even such a basic concept as *word* does not always fit into the structure of non-Indo-European languages. Thus in the Nootka language (spoken by the Indians of Vancouver Island) there is a "word" that denotes *I have been accustomed to eat twenty round objects* (e.g., apples) *while engaged in* (doing so and so).

A faint notion of the rarefied realms in which the Structural Linguists now operate, and the mode in which they write, may be conveyed by a random sampling of their style. This is from *Syntactic Structures* by Dr. Chomsky: "When transformational analysis is properly formulated we find that it is essentially more powerful than description in terms of phrase structure, just as the latter is essentially more powerful than description in terms of finite state Markov processes that generate sentences from left to right." From such passages, which march in sesquipedalian splendor through volume after volume of the expanding bibliography of Structural Linguistics, there have emerged new concepts in the theory of communication, in psychology, epistemology, the theory of signs, cultural anthropology, and the general philosophy of language. But the question many educators and parents are asking today is, How did the concepts of this extremely abstruse discipline come to permeate and affect American education?

To begin with, Bloomfield himself was not content to present his analysis of linguistic structure as an intellectual insight free from social connotations. His studies of Indian tongues coincided in time with the development of egalitarian theories of education, which began to flower in the thirties. Hence in his major work, *Language,* published in 1933, he set forth the idea that insistence on "correct" or "good" English is a form of social snobbery stemming from the British upper classes, perpetuated by the "fanciful doctrine" of grammarians imbued with eighteenth-century authoritarianism, and swallowed by a naïve American public eager to climb the social ladder. He observed that many Americans have a foreign background and "are easily frightened into thinking that a speech form which is natural to them is actually 'not English.'"

The Linguistic credo:
It is undemocratic to attack
"incorrect" English

Although Bloomfield's observations were brief and came at the end of a lengthy scientific work, they had a profound effect on American educators, who during the depression years were eager to help the underprivilegd and eliminate distinctions in the classroom. The idea that the condemnation of "incorrect" usage was undemocratic conformed perfectly to the temper of the nation and also to an educational scene where rigorous teaching methods and standards of achievement were swiftly beginning to sag. The educational theorists, impatient with rote learning, drills, and memory work, were looking for short cuts in every realm. They seized happily, therefore, on Bloomfield's conviction that "correct" English was simply upper-class English, and that to insist on the punctilios of spelling, usage, and diction was to impose harmful class, or status, distinctions on the young.

The developing conflict between the social philosophy of the Structural Linguists and the traditional precepts of grammar might have hung in uneasy balance had it not been for World War II. As the theaters of war expanded around the globe to remote and exotic lands, the government suddenly found itself in need of personnel who could speak not only the familiar languages of Europe but such esoteric tongues as Burmese, Korean, Hausa, Pashto, Fanti, Tagalog, and Thai. Foreseeing this need, a group of linguists attached to the American Council of Learned Societies instituted early in 1941 an intensive program of analysis of little-known tongues. After Pearl Harbor the government called on the Council for help. By the summer of 1942 courses in some twenty-six languages were set up at universities around the country, under the supervision of trained linguistic scientists. Before the war ended the number of foreign tongues taught under various Army programs totaled fifty. Although various methods were employed, newspaper and magazine articles began to speak of the "miraculous" results achieved and gave much of the credit to the new linguistic science. It was at this time that the issue between old and new methods was truly joined. Many progressive schools and colleges began to experiment with the techniques used during the war and to introduce some features of the Army's training program —among them the extensive use of mechanical aids and the techniques of linguistic analysis.

The apostles of Structural Linguistics might still have confined their interest to the teaching of foreign languages had it not been for the extremely influential work of Professor Charles Carpenter Fries of the University of Michigan, a prolific writer who in 1940 published "a scientifically oriented description of actual usage." Entitled *American English Grammar,* it was based on an examination of three thousand letters written to the U.S. War Department in 1918 dealing with the subject of pension money and classified according to the social status of the writers. In 1945 Fries brought forth another book, called *Teaching and Learning English As A Foreign Language.* Applying the principles of Structural Linguistics to English, Fries also embraced Bloomfield's antagonisms toward criteria of speech. He quoted Bloomfield in his preface: "Our schools are conducted by persons who, from professors of education down to teachers in the classroom, know nothing of the results of linguistic science, not even the relation of writing to speech or of standard language to dialect. In short, they do not know what language is, and yet must teach it, and in consequence waste years of every child's life and reach a poor result." To this Fries added, "The views of language that prevail in the schools and among even the 'educated' public still perpetuate the authoritarian attitude of the second half of the eighteenth century and serve to create a huge market for cheap dictionaries and unscholarly handbooks of 'correctness.' "

The principles of Bloomfield, Fries, and their disciples swept the educational field. Borne on the turbulent and chaotic currents of modern pedagogic theory, the teaching of English grammar followed the teaching of Latin into the Dead Sea of abandoned subjects. And as it sank beneath the surface, the linguisticians continued their warfare against all standards of usage anywhere. From Cornell, Dr. Robert A. Hall declared:

It can be just as much of a *faux pas* to say *I saw him,* where your hearer expects and wants *I seen him,* as the other way around. One friend of mine found that when he went to work in a Houston shipyard during the Second World War, he was regarded as a snob for saying *those things* instead of *them things,* and he did not get full co-operation from his fellow workers until he started to say *them things.* . . . What is it that makes some forms "incorrect" and others not? . . . It all boils down really to a question of acceptability. . . . "Correct" can only mean "socially acceptable" and apart from this has no meaning as applied to language.

And from Harvard came an amen from Professor John B. Carroll:

I agree with Hall in rejecting the undemocratic and socially immature attitudes whereby variant and substandard language patterns are condemned; I would even go further and say that pupils should be taught under what circumstances such language patterns can be used appropriately and effectively. Overinsistence on rigid standards of usage may be detrimental to the development of personal styles of oral and written communication.

How to freeze a caste system while professing only the purest democratic principles

To almost everyone who cherishes the English language for its grace and beauty, its combination of precision and flexibility, the social philosophy of the Structural Linguists seems incomprehensible. They epitomize the "anti-intellectualism of the intellectual." For among all the forces of cultural vandalism at work in the country, their work has been the most destructive. The vulgarities of advertising and the avalanches of specialized jargon can be shoveled aside. But the impact of the Structural Linguists is like that of atomic fall-out: through their influence on the schools and on the pupils within them they are incapacitating the coming generation. And the paradoxical aspect of their assault on the English language is that they claim to be motivated only by the purest democratic principles. Recoiling from what they consider the "socio-ethnic snobbery" of graceful speech, they are actually abetting an utterly undemocratic freezing of caste. For if good and correct English—and from here on I shall not enclose either adjective in quotation marks —is regarded as a sign of status, like good manners or expensive clothes, then to commit a language student forever to his own level of speech is surely as undemocratic as denying him the hope of any kind of social or economic advancement. Again and again in the writings of the linguistic philosophers there appears the leitmotiv that language should not be corrected or refined, that everybody should continue to talk the way his parents did, and that any teacher who tries to improve a student's language is endangering the latter's psyche and morale. Commenting on this strange doctrine in a recent article, Joseph Wood Krutch observed:

"Social mobility" is supposed to be one of the glories of our civilization. What becomes of it if the school undertakes to confine every pupil to his own social level? . . . If the purpose of classes in English is not to encourage pupils to speak and write in some fashion different from that which they bring into the classroom with them, then what are these classrooms for? You don't need to go to school to use language in the way your parents and your "group" uses it.

Another blind spot of the Structural Linguists distorts their attitude toward writing. In their preoccupation with speech they painstakingly listen for nuances of sound, slight shadings of stress and juncture and phonemic modification, while professing indifference to matters of literary style, to say nothing of spelling and punctuation. Although no one denies that *Homo sapiens* developed speech before writing, the advent of writing marked the advent of civilization and history. And writing has been the medium by which culture—the accumulated wisdom of the past—has been transmitted down through five millennia since the Sumerians first began to scratch cuneiform symbols on clay tablets in their walled cities on the Tigris-Euphrates plain.

Language is the only vehicle of ideas; if it breaks down, what happens to the ideas?

The Structural Linguists, in their relativisitic approach toward standards of usage, confuse the relationship between language and thought. Concentrated and coherent thought is impossible without the vessel of language in which it is contained. The entity called the mind can conjure up visual images and undergo the turbulence called emotion, but it cannot engender an "idea" without words. This is apparent to professional men involved in government, law, and diplomacy, who know what hazards and disasters can devolve from careless use of language. In these realms the word and its referent are identical. If this were not true, there would be no surrogates' courts to determine how the construction of a subordinate clause or the position of a comma should affect the disposition of a legacy to competing heirs. Nor would there be the necessity of a Supreme Court to interpret the intent of the authors of the Constitution and the interrelationship of its wording with that of state laws or new acts of Congress.

In their attacks on the rigid attitudes of "purists" and "hidebound grammarians" the linguisticians are tilting at windmills. For not even the most rigorous defender of good usage, not even the most embittered critic of the huge dictionary that has become the hostage of Structural Linguistics, has ever contended that the English language is static or will ever be. Every lover of the language knows that its glory resides in the recurring infusions of new elements it has received from all the nations on earth, and that change will never cease. But the written word is the brake on the spoken word. The written word is the link between the past and the future. It demands precision if it is to be the carrier and container of all that is precious in human thought. And along with precision, it can be invested with elegance.

Why the spoken word, which can be gracefully employed only by the exceptionally gifted (Winston Churchill, Charles de Gaulle), should be elevated above the written word is

difficult to conceive. The difference in performance is apparent to anyone who has ever listened to a taped recording of an extemporized speech or read the transcript of a press conference. That the educational system of this country should refrain from teaching students to frame their thoughts in writing, in favor of the kindergarten activities that now occupy their time, should be a cause for national, if not academic, concern.

For the English language has been spreading around the civilized world at an unprecedented rate since World War II. It has become in effect an international language, a lingua franca of trade and commerce, of science and diplomacy, in both hemispheres. The future of civilization may depend on a consensus of thought that can only be achieved by a precise use of English words and a reciprocal comprehension of what they mean. There can be no communication without comprehension. The mechanical media of communication have evolved at a rate which presages the day, not far off, when nations will be able to transmit live television programs across political boundaries and across the seas. If the electronic highways of the air are to serve any useful purpose, however, the content of their signals—the ideas they transmit at the velocity of light—must be garbed in language. And if the English language is permitted to degenerate into a babel of regional dialects, vulgarities, and slang, the hope of any understanding among the millions of English-speaking people around the world is accordingly dimmed. In the health of the English language the health of Western civilization may well reside.

It seems bewildering that, after 2,500 years of an intellectual tradition illuminated by the light of ancient Greece, there should be any need to make a case for clarity of thought and precision of expression. Yet amid the massive onslaught upon intellect and language, waged on so many fronts, it is helpful to recall certain precepts from the past. In the first century A.D. the Roman rhetorician Quintillian set a standard for precision of language when he declared: "One should not aim at being possible to understand, but at being impossible to misunderstand." And more than five centuries earlier the great Chinese philosopher-statesman Confucius expressed his views on the relationship between language and government. Asked what he would undertake to do first, were he called upon to rule a nation, Confucius replied: "To correct language. . . . If language is not correct, then what is said is not what is meant; if what is said is not what is meant, then what ought to be done remains undone; if this remains undone, morals and art will deteriorate; if morals and art deteriorate, justice will go astray; if justice goes astray, the people will stand about in helpless confusion. Hence there must be no arbitrariness in what is said. This matters above everything."

Mr. Barnett has written extensively for Life *on such challenging subjects as the epic of man's history and the grandeur of the natural world. This article in expanded form will serve as the concluding chapter of his book* The Treasure of Our Tongue, *which is to be published next year by Alfred A. Knopf, Inc.*

LEPANTO

By OLIVER WARNER

Threatened by advancing Moslem power, Christian Europe struck back in a last Crusade. For four hours the mightiest fleets hitherto known were locked in desperate battle, and history reached a turning point. For the Catholic West it was the beginning of a brilliant new era; for the Ottoman Turks it was the beginning of the end

The sword of Don John of Austria

LILLY STUNZI—KUNSTHISTORISCHES MUSEUM, VIENNA

There is scarcely a great city in Western Europe—Rome, Madrid, Vienna, Genoa, and Venice notable among them—without its proud memorials of the mighty clash at sea between Christian and Moslem forces that took place near Lepanto on October 7, 1571. It was not only a terrible encounter in itself, it was one of the most picturesque in all sea history. Painters, weavers of tapestry, carvers of trophies-of-arms, engravers of commemorative medals, and jewelers vied with one another to do honor to the Christian victory, the most extraordinary of its kind ever won.

Sea battles may be great in showing the sea commander at his most skillful or resolute; they may be tame and even indecisive as battles, yet important in their effect; or they may be both. Lepanto was great in every sense of the word. It was a milestone in the grim and protracted struggle between the Cross and the Crescent.

It was fought off the shores of Greece, at the entrance to the Gulf of Patras (see map, page 52), and it led to a wave of renewed hope and vigor among the Christian nations. A fleet made up of the forces of the Holy League—Spain, the Papal States, and the Republic of Venice—all under the command of Don John of Austria, defeated the principal fleet of the Turks under Ali Pasha. On the victor's side, notable leaders were the Marqués de Santa Cruz, a Spaniard; Andrea Doria, leading a Genoese squadron; and Marc Antonio Colonna, who commanded the forces of Pius V. It was, in fact as in name, a company drawn from most of Catholic Europe, France excepted.

Lepanto, coming as it did after the repulse of the Turks at the siege of Malta six years earlier, made it certain that the Mediterranean would not become a Moslem lake. Henceforward no sultan would in fact exercise paramount sea power, and although this result was slow to make itself apparent, any further Moslem expansion into the Europe that they had invaded with such success would be mainly at the expense of Poland and Russia. It would be by land. By sea, Spaniards and Italians, with the example before them of the island Knights of Malta, had shown that with leadership, courage, and the help of a new weapon (in this case the heavily gunned galleass) they could withstand the ancient method of fighting solely with oared galleys, manned by slaves.

Don John of Austria, who in the year of Lepanto was not yet twenty-five—though he had already served with distinction against the Moors in Granada—was the natural son of the Emperor Charles V by Barbara Blomberg, the daughter of a wealthy Bavarian. He was thus half brother to Philip II of Spain, one of the pillars of the League; and he had long been, in name at least, the principal Spanish admiral. Fair-haired, eager for fame, Don John proved a good leader for a mixed and quarrelsome fleet.

Among the Italian forces the Venetians, led by Augustino Barbarigo and the veteran Sebastian Veniero, were smarting under the recent loss of most of Cyprus to the Turks, and they bore no love toward the Genoese, their ancient rivals at sea,

led by Giovanni Andrea Doria, nephew of one of Genoa's greatest men. In Doria's squadron a Spanish volunteer was serving whose fame was destined to outshine even that of the commanders. He was Miguel de Cervantes, later to become the author of *Don Quixote*.

The League had been formed in May, 1571, through the tireless efforts of Pope Pius V. This pontiff, who held the See of Rome for only a few years (1566–72), was one of the most memorable figures in an age renowned for great men. Portraits and medals show him with a high forehead, rather sunken eyes, a strong, curved nose, and a pointed beard. He was of humble origin, and even as pope he preferred to continue the ascetic habits of a Dominican monk. His personal piety, zeal, and devotion to the Church have never been exceeded, but he had a gift for diplomacy rare in the saintly. Through his skill and patience he was able to form the first effective combination of Christian forces at a moment that was critical for Europe. His aim was twofold: to bring help to the Venetians, who were losing ground in the eastern Mediterranean, where they had long been the great traders and where they held outposts and possessions; and to prevent the power of the warlike Turk from spreading any closer to the Papal States.

Ever since the tenth century the Turks had been steadily eroding the power of the ancient Christian empire of Byzantium, with its capital at Constantinople. Checked at first by the Crusaders, they became established in Anatolia as early as 1300. Then, crossing first the Black Sea and later the Sea of Marmora into Europe, they began to advance upon the nearer territories of Christendom. The crowning humiliation came in 1453, when Mohammed II took Constantinople itself.

The Turks moved south as well as west. In 1517 Egypt was occupied by Selim I. His successor, Suleiman I, whom men called the Magnificent, extended his sway in the course of a long and splendid reign to Baghdad, to Rhodes, to Belgrade, to Budapest, and almost to the gates of Vienna,

The Victory at Lepanto was painted seventy-eight years after the event, by Georg Wilhelm Graesner, for a parish church in the Calanca Valley of Switzerland—an example of how this "last" Crusade continued to haunt the imagination of Catholic Europe. In the foreground of this detail (in reality, of course, they enjoyed no such vantage point, having remained at home) are the three heads of the Holy League: Philip II of Spain, Pope Pius V, and the Doge of Venice, Luigi Mocenigo. Don John's flagship is directly behind them, and he is probably the man holding aloft the crucifix. The low Turkish vessels are clearly at a disadvantage under the towering galleys of the League.

The illustrations accompanying this article, with the exception of that on page 56, were all photographed by Frau Lilly Stunzi of Zurich. Her interest in Lepanto was first roused by the Ingolstadt monstrance on page 58, and she has since traveled all over Europe in search of materials relating to the battle.

D.   O.   M.
TRIONFO DELLA SEGNA
LATA VITTORIA RIPORTATA
DALL ARMATA CHRISTIANA
CONTRO 300000 TVRCHI. LA PRIMA
DOM.ca D'OTTOBRE L'ANNO 15 71
NELLA QVALE DA 20000 CHRIST
IANI FVRONO AMMAZATI 32000 T
VRCHI PIV DE 3600 FATTI SCHIAVI
RESTANDO SOLO 2000 CHRISTIANI DI
PINTA PER ORDINE, ET A' SPESA DI
TVTTA LA COMPAGNIA DEL SANT
ISSIMO ROSARIO ERETTA IN QVESTA
CHIESA DI SANTA MARIA DETTA
DI CALANCHA

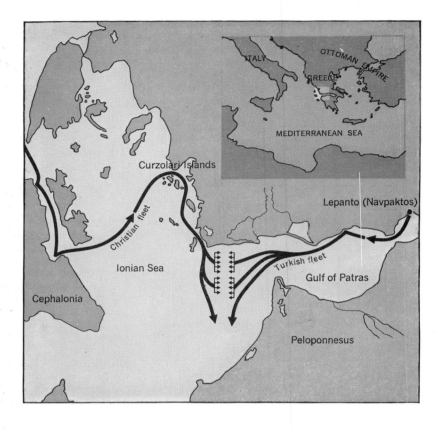

Lepanto was one of the last great naval battles to be fought in the old way, with the fleets lined up in rigid formation and meeting each other head-on. The modern map at left, however, shows that two wings —the Christian right and the Turkish left—quickly broke away to the south in an attempt to outflank each other. The contemporary engraving opposite gives no hint of this, although it purports to be the "true order of the Christian and Turkish fleets" as of 5 P.M. Actually, by then the battle was over and Don John was (or would be when the news got back) the hero of Christendom. His feat—and features—were soon marked by the medal above.

capital of the Holy Roman emperors who ruled most of Western Europe. To this day Hungarians remember the defeat of Mohács, fought less than half a century before Lepanto, as one of the saddest in their history, although much later they had their revenge on the very same field.

The Turks were united. They were bred to arms. They upheld the great cause of Islam. Only by following their example of unity and devotion, only by reviving a spiritual fire that seemed to have been damped since the Crusades, could the Christians hope to stem the tide.

If the Christians found the necessary inspiration in the noble and determined character of the Pope, they were hardly less fortunate in their tactical leader. Don John of Austria was one of those rare men who seem to have been born with a gift for war. He had been brought up in Spain, and was recognized very early by Philip II as a young man to whom responsible posts could be entrusted; and his age, his birth, and his experience against the corsairs of North Africa and the Moors in Granada all seemed to fit him to lead the great armada which the efforts of Pius V had assembled.

Don John's original rendezvous was to be at Messina. When he arrived there, he found himself in charge of more than three hundred ships, two thirds of them known as royal galleys, each with a nominal complement of one hundred soldiers in addition to the rowers who toiled at the oars.

The Spanish contingent was the largest: eighty galleys, twenty-two other vessels, and no less than twenty-one thousand fighting men. The Venetians contributed more than a hundred vessels, but most were poorly manned, and their six heavily armed galleasses were in fact the Republic's most important asset. These galleasses, which were towed into action by lighter vessels, were broader in the beam than the galley; the additional depth allowed the erection, forward, of a structure, fitted with swivel guns, that anticipated the modern armored turret.

In the galleass the usual ornamental stem of the galley was replaced by a formidable point, while lower down the solid cutwater, or prow, was effective against anything of smaller size that could not get out of the way. Sides and stern were also heavily armed, while the rowers were protected by a deck that served as a platform for the fighting men. In battle the rowers were yoked in both directions, some pulling and some pushing at the fifty-foot oars.

The Pope himself fitted out twelve galleys, hired many more, and supplied the necessary troops. No less than eighty thousand men assembled at Messina with his official blessing. Of

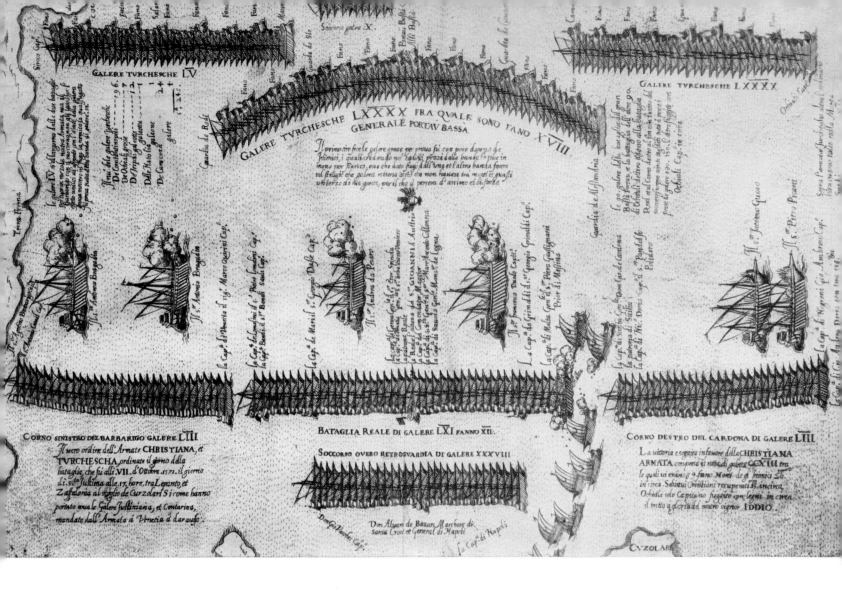

these, some fifty thousand volunteers, impressed men, and slaves labored at the oars. The rest were soldiers. Don John, with the aid of a blackboard, explained his methods to representatives of the fighting men, gave the captains of his fleet detailed information as to how he would meet the most likely tactical contingencies, and arranged for appropriate signals.

While he was surveying and ordering his fleet, he got news that the Turks, who were believed to have massed about three hundred ships, were roving the Ionian Sea and attacking the islands therein. On September 16 the Christians put to sea, and the first precise news of the enemy came before the end of the month, when Don John anchored off Corfu. There he learned that the Turkish commander, Ali Pasha, had recently landed, burned some churches, failed to subdue the island's fortress, and had then retreated to the anchorage of Lepanto, which was far up the eighty-mile stretch of water now known as the Gulf of Corinth.

At a council of war, characterized like many such councils by acrimony and dispute, those who were for instant attack carried the day. They included Colonna, Barbarigo, Santa Cruz, and Don John himself. The season was growing late, and the differences between the Allies, never far from the surface, were increasing. Spaniards and Venetians had already

come to blows, largely due to the fact that Spaniards had to be drafted into the Venetian ships to bring them up to strength.

Off Cephalonia, on October 6, a ship from Crete brought news of the fall of Famagusta, the last Venetian stronghold in Cyprus, and of the torture and death of its noble defenders. A wave of horror spread through the Allies, and an immediate advance was ordered into waters where the enemy was known to be waiting. One further item of news was not altogether cheering. It appeared that Ali Pasha had been reinforced by the ships of Uluch Ali, once a Calabrian fisherman but now the dey of Algiers and known to be a daring corsair by many in the Christian fleet.

During the night of October 6 the Turks, with a favoring wind, advanced westward toward the Christians. At dawn on October 7 the most powerful forces that had ever met at sea came within sight of one another at the entrance to the Gulf of Patras, which is west of the larger Gulf of Corinth.

Here, as at most earlier naval battles, fleets met like armies. Their formation was rigid; the commands were military; and tactics were based upon experience by land. The sailors got the ships where they were wanted, while the "generals" and their soldiers fought it out.

Before he drew up his formal line of battle, Don John gave

TEXT CONTINUED ON PAGE 57

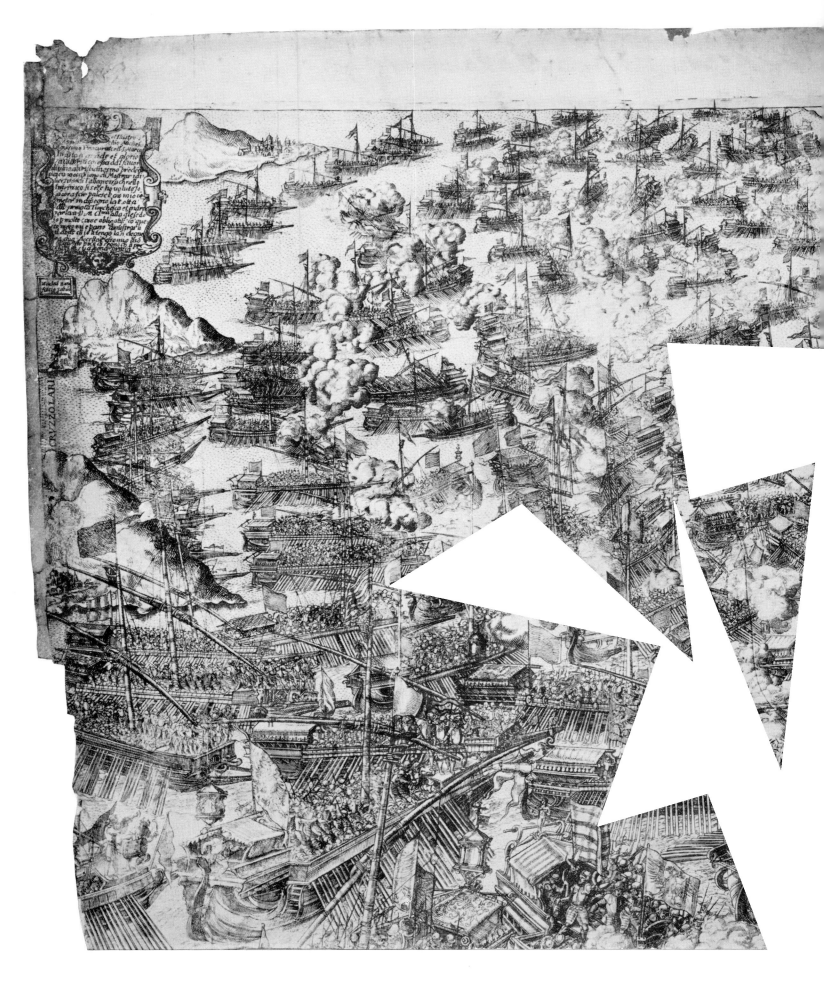

This congested scene of carnage—one can hardly see the ships for the oars—is a panorama of Lepanto executed in 1572 by the Venetian engraver Ferrando Bertelli. Although no doubt somewhat fanciful, it does give an idea of what naval warfare was like in the sixteenth century. The decks of the galleys are jammed with armed soldiers; beneath them, unseen

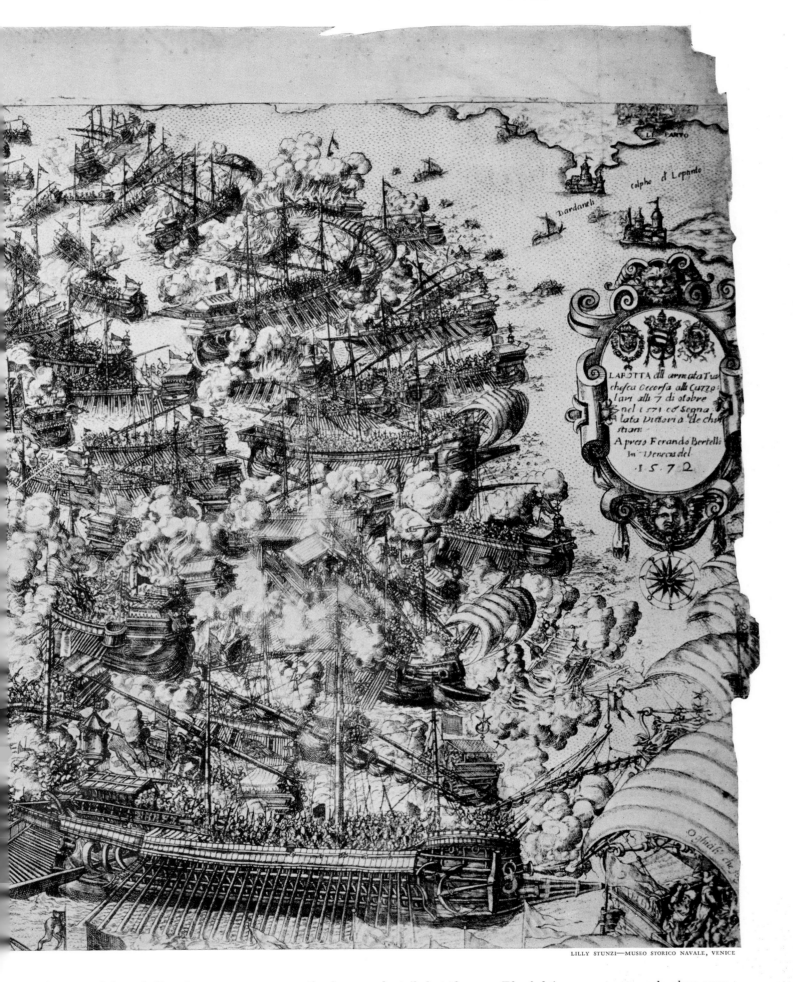

but essential, are half again as many men—mostly slaves—who toiled at the oars. The fighting was at extremely close quarters and often took the form of hand-to-hand combat. It is difficult to distinguish the Christians from the Turks, but Don John is the slightly outsize figure shown in a heroic stance left of center and just above the bottom margin.

two orders. The first was to remove the iron beaks which protruded ten or fifteen feet from the bows of certain of the fighting ships. The second was that no one should fire "until near enough to be splashed with the blood of an enemy." Both directives were wise. The battle would not be won by ramming, but by close fighting, in which the Spaniards' armor, together with their arquebuses, might prove a decisive advantage.

Barbarigo and his Venetians were placed on the left wing, Barbarigo himself sailing as close as he dared to the inshore rocks and shoals, in the hope that his flank could not be turned. Andrea Doria was on the right wing, where papal galleys were mingled with the Genoese. In the center was the flagship of Don John, conspicuous by its high, carved poop and triple-stern lanterns, its green pennant at the forepeak, and its Holy Standard at the maintop. Near him were Veniero and Colonna. In reserve were thirty-five Spanish and Venetian galleys under Santa Cruz, ready to apply their strength where most needed.

As the fleets neared each other the six Venetian galleasses, the spearhead of the Christian attack, were towed into position. Two, in line ahead, were placed in front of each main squadron. When every preparation had been made, Don John boarded a fast vessel and sailed behind the three-mile front across which his forces extended, heartening his men and, in his turn, being cheered.

By the time Don John had returned to his own galley, the wind had changed in his favor. He was now able to see that the Turks had their fleet arrayed in the form of a huge crescent, but this was altered, almost at once, to conform to his own dispositions. There were many Christian galley slaves in the Turkish fleet. To them Ali Pasha said: "If I win the battle, I promise you your liberty. If the day is yours, then God has given it to you."

First blood was drawn by the galleasses of Don John's center. Their guns, heavier than anything the Turks possessed, did their execution at long range, sinking several Turkish galleys even before the main forces were in contact. Partly as a result of this initial setback the left and right wings of the Moslems separated from the center. Uluch Ali made a wide sweep toward the southern shore, in an attempt to outflank Andrea Doria, while Mohammed Sirocco held a similar course toward Barbarigo and the northern shore. Ali Pasha's center squadron, eluding the powerful galleasses as best it could, drove on to meet that of Don John. By midday, or shortly after, the two flagships were locked together, crossbow and arquebus being exchanged for sword and scimitar, the decks slippery with blood from close fighting. And by that time, all three squadrons were at grips.

Against the Christian left, Sirocco's maneuver succeeded. His knowledge of the shore line enabled him to sail even closer to it than Barbarigo, and to surround him. The Venetian admiral was attacked by eight Turkish galleys, and he himself was killed by an arrow. Twice the Venetian flagship was stormed; twice it was retaken. At last, when help came from

Several Turkish vessels, with their rich panoply of flags, pennants, and silken tents, may be seen in the foreground of the detail opposite (from a painting of the Venetian school). Some of these captured banners still hang in the churches and museums of Western Europe. But of the Turkish admiral himself, Ali Pasha, we have neither relics nor biography (Ali is a common Moslem name and Pasha, of course, a title). The portrait above is imaginary. It was published in Nuremberg as a broadside some nine years after he lost the battle and—as here gloatingly depicted—his head.

The climax came when Don John gave the order to board: once, twice, parties were driven back, but at last they carried the Turkish poop. There Ali Pasha, already wounded in the head, tried to buy his life with a promise of treasure. It was in vain. Even his protective talisman, the right canine tooth of Mohammed contained in a crystal ball, did not avail him. A soldier cut him down, hacked off his head, and carried it to Don John. The admiral, recoiling in horror, ordered the man to throw the grisly trophy into the sea. But the Spaniard disobeyed him and mounted it on a pike, which was then held aloft in the prow of the Turkish flagship. Consternation spread among the Moslems, and within a few moments resistance was over. The Ottoman standard, inscribed with the name of Allah twenty-nine thousand times and never before lost in battle, was lowered from the maintop. Don John was then able to turn his attention to his right wing, where all was not well.

No less than five of Doria's galleys had been stricken. On the *San Giovanni* and the *Piamontesa* virtually everyone was dead. The *Doncella* was not much better off, while in the *Florence* only the captain and seventeen seamen survived out of two hundred. The *Marquesa* was also hard pressed. It was in this ship that Cervantes was serving. He had been ill with fever before the battle, but he had risen from his sickbed and had volunteered for a place of danger. There he remained throughout the battle and received the wound that disabled his left hand for life.

Uluch Ali, whose Algerians had done most of the damage on the Christian right, retreated to the shelter of Lepanto where he learned of the death of Ali Pasha, although sixteen of his galleys turned on their pursuers and fought one of the bloodiest encounters of the entire day with Don Juan of Cardona. But as the four-hour fight came to a close, with the enemy center and right almost totally destroyed and the left in gradual retreat, Don John at last had time to survey the action as a whole and to begin to reckon his gain and loss.

Nearly eight thousand of the bravest men in Spain and Italy were dead; double that number were wounded. The Turks and Algerians lost at least three times as many killed, and some twelve thousand Christian slaves were rescued from their galleys. Never again did the Turkish sultan contrive to assemble so powerful a fleet. Christians and Turks had been roughly equal in numbers, and had fought with equal courage. Victory went to the side with better weapons and better leadership; here the galleass and the person of Don John proved decisive.

Lepanto was Don John's first and last major sea battle. He

Canale and others, Sirocco's ship was sunk and he was thrown into the water. Although by then badly wounded, he was rescued, only to be beheaded on the spot by his captors.

On the Christian right the battle had at first gone equally badly. Although Uluch Ali had not been able to outflank Andrea Doria, he had at once doubled back to a gap that had opened in the Allied line and had taken part of Don John's squadron in the rear. Among the ships attacked was the *Capitana* of Malta, commanded by Giustiniani, Prior of the Order of Saint John. The Prior fell with five arrows in his body, and the *Capitana* was made prize. At the most critical time Santa Cruz, seeing the Maltese in tow of the enemy, moved to the rescue, and Uluch Ali, relinquishing his capture, made haste to retreat.

The issue was decided in the center. Here, from the first, the virtue of Don John's order to dismantle the iron beaks had been clear. The Turkish admiral had not done this, and though the forepeak of his flagship towered over the Christian decks, his forecastle guns fired into the air. Those of Don John, placed at a lower level, riddled the Turkish galley with shot just above her water line. The armored Spanish arquebusiers soon decimated the Turkish ranks. Not for nothing were the Spaniards reckoned the steadiest soldiers of their time.

to bring Europe to the proud splendor of the flowering of the Baroque age. Vaults, cupolas, and arches, which had originated in the architecture of Imperial Rome and been modified in Byzantium, reappeared in great buildings, replacing the slender, mystical dreaminess of later Gothic buildings. There was a new, rich solidity of horizontal planes, and polychromatic exuberance in metal and marbles. All betokened renewal of belief in life, religion, art, and politics.

To be sure, Lepanto did not end Turkish power and aspiration, or even destroy Turkish sea power. More than seventy years later the Turks mounted an invasion of Crete, which was one of the main Venetian outposts. The siege began in 1645 and continued over two decades, Candia holding out against all attacks until at last attrition and hunger took their toll and the fortress fell. The Turks continued their struggle with the Holy Roman emperors of Vienna, the capital being once again endangered in 1683 and saved only by an astonishing rescue march by John Sobieski, Poland's hero-king, who rendered a unique service in the old chivalrous spirit to a fellow Christian ruler.

What Lepanto proved was that Turkish power could be contained, and that the Crescent was not invincible. It was as profound in its effects as, for instance, were the battles of Stalingrad and Midway in the last great war. It was the beginning of a long and lasting revival. Christendom had found the will and strength to push back the invader; memories of the Crusades came flooding back; and as Cervantes grew older, more mature, and more experienced, he wrote that affectionate monument to Christian chivalry, *Don Quixote.*

died in the Low Countries at the age of thirty-one, a man of one paramount success and many disappointments. Like the galleys he commanded, he belonged to an old order of sea warfare, one whose history went back to the days of Actium, Salamis, and beyond. The future was with sail, with the broadsides of the future ships of the line.

The "tumult and the shouting" died, the "captains and the kings" departed, the fleet dispersed, the squadrons on regular service took up new dispositions, the wounded went home to die or to be cared for; and then, slowly but surely, the news of the action spread far and wide. In the sixteenth century events took a long time to fit into a proper perspective—yet there were compensations. Great happenings made more impact than anything we hear as news today, except in the rarest circumstances. Men and women gave every episode and incident its full value, and survivors of Lepanto would tell their tales to enraptured audiences in every corner of Europe.

The cumulative impact was both astounding and permanent. The victory may be said to have begun a spirit of revival—in war, diplomacy, the arts, and architecture—which was in time

PHILIPPO MAXIMO HISPANIARVM ET MAXIMAR
DE CRVC LEGATVS SVVS APVD

By RICHARD MOSS

A PAIR
OF
DESIGNING
FINNS

The Scandinavian talent for shaping common objects wi

The Finnish forest forms a background to the lives of the artist and craftsman Tapio Wirkkala and (peering over his shoulder) his artist-craftsman wife, Rut Bryk. In a country famous for its designers, they have achieved an unusual degree of fame. In a land where nature is never far away, they manage to be urbane, sophisticated artisans without losing touch with Finland's icy solitudes. The Wirkkalas live part of the year in the remote far north, part of it in an apartment outside Helsinki. On the window sill of the latter, refracting the marshy landscape outside (opposite below) are a group of crystal paperweights designed by Wirkkala, one with an air bubble inside.

:votion and elegant style has found new master craftsmen in Tapio Wirkkala and his wife

Since the coming of the Industrial Revolution, traditional handicrafts have tended to degenerate into either a bohemian affectation, occupational therapy, or an adjunct of the tourist trade. But this is not so in Scandinavia, where the national craft traditions have been adapted to industry, and industry to them—and especially is it not so in Finland. The Finns have not only conserved their handicrafts but have retained a sense of them as natural, harmonious elements in an active and productive life.

Among the most inventive of Finnish designer-craftsmen are Tapio Wirkkala and his wife, Rut Bryk. In the city of Helsinki, where designers are as common as brokers in Wall Street, they are perhaps the best known. Their work has been shown in many exhibitions in Europe and several in the United States (one, a few years ago, by the Smithsonian Institution). When Georg Jensen, the firm of Danish silversmiths, set up the Lunning Prize for outstanding Scandinavian designers in 1951, it was no surprise that Wirkkala was chosen for the first award.

Close though their lives are, the talents of the two Wirkkalas lie along different lines, and their studios are on opposite sides of town. Wirkkala rejoices in form and texture, but with a certain objectivity; he lets them speak for themselves. His wife's designs are more personally expressive. Where his delight is in materials, hers is in color; she works mainly in fabrics and ceramics, for which she has won numerous prizes, including a Grand Prix at Milan in 1951.

Her studio is atop the Arabia porcelain factory, which is enlightened enough to support her as a resident craftsman. His, a merrily cluttered establishment in downtown Helsinki, is provided for him by A. Ahlström, a wide-ranging industrial trust that commissions and manufactures more than half his designs. Both arrangements are typical of the way in which Finnish industry and Finnish craftsmen work together. Originally trained as a graphic designer (he did stamps and bank notes for the government), Wirkkala entered a competition held after the war by the Karhula-Iittala Glassworks, a subsidiary of Ahlström. Though he had never worked in glass before, he came away with the top prizes and is today one of Karhula-Iittala's chief designers.

If Tapio Wirkkala were a dozen years older (he is forty-eight), he would doubtless be known as the Grand Old Man of contemporary Finnish design. He has left his mark on almost every category of domestic equipment—furniture, lighting, crockery, glassware, silver, and the rest. In a country that demands versatility of its artisans, the effortless ease with which Wirkkala handles such diverse materials as porcelain, glass, wood, and metals goes far beyond the ordinary. It would be hard to pigeonhole him: he is at the same time artist, craftsman, and industrial designer—he speaks of his career as "a mixed salad." Some of his works are purely decorative *objets d'art;* others might be used to hold flowers or cigarette ashes, depending on the whim of the user; still others are as unquestionably utilitarian as light bulbs.

Silhouetted against the Lapland sky (right) the Finnish designer Wirkkala tugs at his pipe and contemplates what seems to be melting ice but is really a piece of glass in the slaglike form it often takes when the furnace cools. Wirkkala has become especially well-known for his glass, and works in it eloquently, sometimes etching it, as in his Madonna *(below), with its startling infant and menacing demons copper-engraved on an inch-thick cross, and sometimes molding it to serve as flower holders—or any other use that might occur to you—in severe icelike shapes (as at far right) appearing to be only shortly removed from those of nature.*

A unique piece of art glass formed by the artist himself and a set of design drawings for crockery to be turned out by a factory in great numbers are altogether different items. But for Wirkkala they are two instruments for playing the same music. Both are exercises in giving form to material, in creating something out of nothing, which is chiefly what he likes to do. "We are like children," he says, "always playing." Whatever the purpose of his designs, they all bear a common stamp. All are basically functional, though their forms go beyond mere functionalism for its own sake, achieving a blend of hinterland vigor and seaside sophistication that seems especially appropriate in Finland. For this is a country in which the backwoods come down almost to the coast. A hearty robustness modulated into cultivated, urbane forms is what characterizes Wirkkala's work: it is his style, just as it is the man himself. A keen, well-traveled intelligence is hidden within his self-effacing, almost brooding, north-country reticence; and cosmopolitan tastes continually look out from behind his burly features and his outdoorsman's twinkle.

All Finns are apparently votaries of nature. They refuse to bulldoze it out of the way. For example, the Wirkkalas and their two children live for most of the year in a duplex apartment on the outskirts of Helsinki in what—for any other country—would be the suburbs. Yet you would hardly know it from the landscape; from their living-room windows the Wirkkalas look out—not on the wreckage of urban

The difficulty of defining Wirkkala is emphasized by the contrast between his highly original sculpture in laminated birchwood (above) and the table setting (below) of a silver pattern, for which he won an international award. Yet the echo of the Finnish woodlands still remains. Striations of alternating layers of birchwood and glue, then carved and sanded, give his sculpture its suggestion of a Brancusi bird about to take flight; while under the silver is a mat, also of Wirkkala's own design, made of alternating strips of light and dark wood.

Even though they are attractive enough to be used without shades, Wirkkala's light bulbs (below) represent an aspect of his industrial design that contrasts with the work of his wife. Rut Bryk is especially known for her laatat, ceramic plaques on which she paints in glaze. Her subjects are sometimes semi-mythological beasts (like the lion at left), sometimes enormous flowers, episodes from Finnish folklore, or canal-side Venetian palaces (the Wirkkalas travel frequently to Italy). On the plaques her colors, forming in glassy pools where the clay is indented, are generally somber—meditative and winterlike—while on her fabrics or her tiles (opposite) they break into a riot of autumnal yellows, reds, ambers, and golds. Sometimes the mood of her designs is fanciful, sometimes mystical, but always strange and compelling. She has found a vocabulary suited to herself in a style that might be called Finnish Gothic.

sprawl—but on the gray creek waters and sedge-covered salt marshes of the Baltic seacoast.

The rudeness of the soil and the inhospitable climate have only drawn the Finns even closer to their land. "Take a piece of ice in the hand," says Wirkkala, in a rare but characteristically romantic utterance, "and find our culture from it. Find it in a stone smoothed by the rapids, or in sand designed by the waves." Find it in Lapland. A few years ago Wirkkala acquired an abandoned log cabin in the far north, and he and his family now spend their summers there. From Helsinki it is four hours due north by plane, another four hours by car through the forests, and another four hours by motorboat across Lake Inari. And it is easier to get in, the Wirkkalas report, than out.

Here, beyond the Arctic Circle, the Wirkkalas fish for their food, cook over an open fireplace, and sleep on benches covered with reindeer skins. The crisp slant light of the unsetting sun, the silences of the pine forests, the expanses of still water, the low-lying primeval hills, reduce life to its essentials—and, for the Wirkkalas, to its essential abundance. Their craft is rooted in nature like a tree, and it is no wonder that the unembellished plenitude they find in Lapland should show itself so abundantly in their work.

Richard Moss, a former editor of Industrial Design, *went to Finland for* HORIZON *specially to interview the Wirkkalas.*

THE LITERARY
PRIZE GAME

Medals, ribbons, citations, or good hard cash—awards for

writers are the objects of subtle but very energetic politicking

By DAVID DEMPSEY

The story is told of an eminent poet who appeared not long ago at a state dinner without wearing any of his eleven medals. Instead, on his jacket was pinned a small sign: "See catalogue." Such a sporting attitude, however apocryphal it may be, is not typical of most writers today, among whom prize fever is endemic. Although few winners actually wear their decorations, or mount plaques over the fireplace, there is a trophy room—or at least room for a trophy—in the mind of every author who takes his art seriously. And why not? The literary prize has become the writer's merit badge, proof that he has succeeded as a man of letters.

In view of this it is not surprising that a new kind of politics has grown up, that of prize getting; and with it a new breed of writer, the professional prize winner. This is strikingly a product of our own times. A seventy-nine-page directory of literary awards published in 1935 has grown, in its 1963 edition, to two hundred eighty pages. As patrons of the arts increase (thanks in part to the income tax), so does the patronage. With a businesslike efficiency that could well be the envy of the French National Lottery, some seventy organizations in this country dispense about a hundred literary awards and grants annually. Many of these are trivial. Others are consolation prizes which, in effect, reward the failures rather than the successes of a publishing season. And some are nothing if not

exotic: The American Historical Association biennially awards the Watumull Prize (worth $500) for the best history of India originally published in the United States, an incentive that has usually assured readers a history of India every two years since the prize was set up in 1945. Columbia University administers a fund (the Loubat) that provides a prize every five years of $1,200 for, among other subjects, the best book on the "numismatics of North America."

A writer competing for the Athenaeum Literary Award has a special problem. He can write about anything he chooses, but he must arrange to live "within thirty miles of the Philadelphia City Hall" at the time his book is written or published. For twenty-six years Hart Schaffner & Marx, the men's clothing manufacturer, gave book awards. Don't laugh. The "take" ran as high as $5,000, and before the prizes were discontinued fifty-three volumes—mostly on economics—had received the H. S. & M. label. To win a literary award, in fact, one need not write a book at all; a librarian can do it for "outstanding professional achievement in cataloguing and classification."

Nevertheless, the major prizes—the Pulitzer, the National Book Awards, the Bancroft in History, the Bollingen in Poetry, and the awards voted annually by the National Institute of Arts and Letters—carry sufficient prestige, and in some cases enough cash booty, to make prize getting worthwhile. Writers may scoff at the system in private, but with the single exception of Sinclair Lewis, who refused the Pulitzer in 1926 for *Arrowsmith*—

he objected to the criteria set forth in the Pulitzer will—no American author has ever declined an important award when it came his way.

In an ordinary, or "good," year the total monetary value of these prizes is about $80,000. Winnings are tax free. Increased sales of award-winning books may also produce a few thousand dollars more in royalties. Occasionally, too, there is a "great" year, when the kitty will be swelled by unexpected largess. This happened most recently in 1959, when the Ford Foundation decanted $150,000 on a group of eleven American poets and novelists, two of whom were then past sixty. The remarkable thing about these gifts is that they were not given for works already published, or even necessarily in progress, but simply for books the authors might wish to write. There was no obligation to produce anything. At such times as this the profession of letters seems almost attractive.

To most serious writers it seldom does, in the economic sense at least, and this may explain why so many of them willingly submit to the ceremonial agony of receptions and prize-giving dinners. The knowledge that someone cares, that one's work has been recognized, is important. Ego is an author's venture capital.

Proof of this takes curious forms. "Would you be so kind as to send me," wrote John Steinbeck to the administrative director of the National Institute of Arts and Letters some few years ago, "any medal, ribbon or ceremonial sword which would fit my academic grandeur? I am tired of seeing Marc Connelly covered with decorations, strutting like a peacock, while I have no more ornaments than a flycatcher."

A rosette was promptly dispatched to Steinbeck, to be pinned in his lapel; and should he have chosen to do so, he could also have sported "a purple and gold ribbon worn diagonally from the right shoulder to the waist" (the Institute's insignia). Steinbeck can afford to poke fun at America's leading cathedral of culture—his books make money, and he has won the Nobel Prize. Few authors are as fortunate, and may they not be pardoned if the crumbs brushed off on them from the festive table of best-sellerdom happen to be gold, or gold-plated?

Yet only the naïve can suppose that the medals and money necessarily fall into the hands of the deserving. The politics of prize giving is a subtle one. The truth is that most prizes are not given but sold. As the patrons of literature multiply, it becomes increasingly clear that there is an award for every type of writer who is willing to perform. The State of Texas gets its prized historians, natural history its laureates; and every cause can be assured of at least one ardent defender. With fiction writers it pays to conform to the literary fashion of the day; maverick novelists, such as Norman Mailer, for example, are not highly regarded by prize juries. It helps to be established: many organizations that give awards do so chiefly for the prestige that accrues to *them*. And it does no harm to be a joiner—societies have a weakness for honoring their own members. One should not be an expatriate, nor should one seriously question the basic political mores of his country; extreme leftists, for instance, have a way of being left out when

the plaques and loving cups are handed around.

But the most influential force that a writer can have working for him is a good cheering section. With the Nobel Prize this is indispensable: an author must be nominated—by an academy, university, or a group of writers—and the more frequently he is nominated, the better are his chances. "It has happened that perseverance wins," a booklet issued by the Swedish Academy states disingenuously. Likewise, numerous awards in this country will frequently go to the writer with the most friends in court. Sometimes this is the public itself—perhaps the surest way to be eligible for a Pulitzer Prize is to write a best seller—but more often it is a lobby of peers intent upon aiding one of their colleagues. This may not be downright intrigue, as some writers have insisted, but the situation has produced some odd results. Three out of every four prize-winning authors are men. And if they are poets, it is more than likely that they will be rather elderly men.

With poetry, the rewards of prizemanship are most pronounced. It has been remarked that although most poets go unread, few go unscrolled. One might suppose, therefore, that the beneficence of juries would filter down to the bright young talents who, more than their elders, need recognition if they are to stay in the race. But such is seldom the case: if writing verse is a young man's fancy, being rewarded for it has become an old man's game. The late Edgar Lee Masters was "cited" with a $5,000 fellowship from the Academy of American Poets at the age of seventy-seven. He was fortunate. Edwin Markham was eighty-five—thirty-eight years had elapsed since the publication of "The Man With the Hoe"—when he was similarly rewarded. The average age of *all* Academy fellows, at the time of their appointment, has been just short of seventy-two years. The Bollingen Prize, administered by Yale University, has done better: its winners have averaged a vigorous sixty. Even the National Book Awards Committee, which prides itself on breaking with tradition, has not been able to get the figure below fifty-four.

It is clear that we are getting a gerontocracy of poets in America, and it is equally plain that our prize system is the culprit. An astonishing number of these poets are themselves members of the juries (see chart on page 72) that decide on who shall be crowned. (With but three exceptions in fourteen years of prize giving, the National Book Award has gone to poets who have at one time or another served on N.B.A. juries.) Like circuit riders of old, the judges allocate their time to different prize committees, the appointments changing from year to year. In general they represent the "modern" school of poetry, and outsiders have a hard time breaking in, as the traditionalist Karl Shapiro has discovered.

This does not mean that prize winners write bad poetry. An inventory of the late Robert Frost's estate would reveal medals and plaques representing seventeen major awards, including four Pulitzers. (Runner-up Archibald MacLeish has won eleven prizes; Marianne Moore, ten; and Carl Sandburg, nine.) Frost was an exception to the superannuation principle—he went on writing to the end, and what is more, made a living at it—but for a poet, he was no mean politician. A gregarious man with a hearty appetite, he traveled the prize circuit for years, cheerfully aware that part of the cost of doing business was one's presence at a dinner.

This is accomplished, in most cases, on a *quid pro quo* basis reminiscent of the Renaissance, when patrons were patrons and poets sang for their supper.* For example, the Academy of American Poets holds an annual banquet, usually at the Waldorf-Astoria. This is a dress-up occasion, attended by some nine hundred guests from the world of Business, Society, and the Arts. Emphasis is on affairs of state—perhaps out of nostalgic respect for Shelley's poet as "unacknowledged legislator." A typical program in 1959 included addresses by the British Representative to the United Nations, the President of the Rockefeller Institute for Medical Research, and the then Secretary of Health, Education, and Welfare. Miss Léonie Adams, who in 1954 had a busy year winning three prizes, appeared to accept the latest $5,000 fellowship—the largest in the United States that is reserved exclusively for poets.

Meeting in the same hotel, a few days later, the Poetry Society of America drew only four hundred diners, but made up for its second-place showing in attendance by awarding more prizes—thirteen, collectively worth $2,650. There was compensation, too, in the fact that no mere cabinet member, but the President himself addressed the gathering, albeit *in absentia*. Eisenhower's views on the importance of poetry must have been interesting to some of the more sophisticated guests, in the light of a booklet published shortly before by *Good Housekeeping* that purported to include his favorite poems. Among these were "Old Ironsides," "Little Boy Blue," and "The Old Oaken Bucket."

The point in both instances is that the poet has become someone to be vaguely honored rather than seriously read. What began as a prize of discovery has become the prize of consecration; and men who refuse to exchange vine leaves for a dinner jacket—beatniks like Lawrence Ferlinghetti, no matter how impoverished, and eccentrics such as the late Robinson Jeffers, no matter how elderly—are passed over in favor of the poet who is willing to play the game.

The big prizes today are given almost entirely for past achievement. These are the so-called "career" awards, and by their very nature, they nearly always go to a writer after he has gained wide public recognition—sometimes long after. From the judges' point of view such prizes are "safe." They seldom get anyone into trouble. The Bollingen, for example, inaugurated with such high promise in 1949 and now worth $2,500, has proved to be another means of endowing excellence that needs no endowment. Among its recipients have been W. H. Auden, Archibald MacLeish, Conrad Aiken, and e. e. cummings. This is also true of the Huntington Hartford Foundation awards in "creativity," which carry a stipend of $5,000 and six months' residence at the Foundation's estate in California. Hartford buys no cut-rate merchandise. His grantees include Max Eastman, Mark Van Doren, Robert Frost, Van Wyck Brooks, and Conrad Aiken. Obviously these men, who averaged seventy-two years of age at the time of their appointment, are all eminent writers. But they are also among the insiders who have come to dominate the field of prize getting.

Even the National Institute of Arts and Letters, and its upper house, the American Academy of Arts and Letters—a select "inner" group comprising fifty of the Institute's membership of two hundred fifty—has not entirely escaped this rear-view syndrome, and one of its awards is specifically earmarked "for an older person."

Occupying a mammoth granite complex, on West 155th Street in New York, which it shares with the Museum of the American Indian, the Institute is virtually a prize factory, passing out a minimum of twenty-eight awards and grants each year. (In addition to literature, prizes are given in architecture, painting, sculpture, drama, music, and "good speech on the stage.") It is nothing, however, if not democratic; nominees for the various literary honors are chosen by a committee of seven, but winners of some of the awards are elected by a majority vote of the Institute's members. Lobbyists can have a field day in the Institute, if they are so inclined, but a more practical factor is the predisposition, aesthetic and otherwise, of the nominating committee. Of the current group of seven judges in literature, three are either staff members or regular contributors to *The New Yorker*. Their choices, not surprisingly, tend to reflect a rather sophisticated point of view—Faulkner, John Updike, Cozzens, and Aldous Huxley are among recent winners—but in any case popular appeal is by no means a criterion; indeed, one of the Academy's prizes is by definition limited to a novel of merit that "is not a commercial success."

Like most academies, too, this one enjoys a pleasant narcissism; since 1910 a Gold Medal has been presented for "distinguished achievement" in literature. All but four of the thirty-four medals awarded to date have gone to an Institute member. (Average age at the time: sixty-two.)

Despite the critical buffeting to which it has been subjected during its forty-six-year history, the Pulitzer is still the most prestigious prize in American letters: the $500 payoff is secondary to the journalistic fuss that accrues to the winner. With its built-in publicity mechanism—all but two of the Pulitzer members of the advisory board are newspaper editors—the annual prizes are front-page stories all over the country. (Announcements of other literary awards have a way of ending up on page

18.) The effect of a Pulitzer, if not the intention, is that of a lifetime appointment, for the pleasing alliterative slogan that gets fastened to a winner's name becomes a valuable trademark on all subsequent books.

To win a Pulitzer an author should address himself to a comfortable, middlebrow audience that believes, as Joseph Pulitzer himself did, in comfortable American uplift. It does not always work out this way, of course; nor has this caveat prevented some excellent books from getting the prize. But as a generalization it can be said that for a poet to win he should be "readable" —i.e., not too modern; a biographer should expand on the Founding Fathers or an equally eminent political figure, long dead (and if he expands to two volumes, so much the better), while a playwright must be able to show a comfortable run at the box office.

A novelist's chances are enhanced if he has turned out a best seller, or achieved such indubitable literary stature that he can no longer be safely ignored. Measured from *The Sun Also Rises*, published in 1926, it took the Pulitzer Advisory Board twenty-seven years to discover Hemingway; Ellen Glasgow won with her twenty-third novel, Upton Sinclair with his forty-seventh.

If this is a weakness, perhaps the fault is partly with the publishers: only books submitted are eligible for judging; and publishers, by and large, have an understandable fondness for entering their commercial favorites rather than the offbeat work that has a limited potential audience. Economics may thus be the principal arbiter.

In any case the judges operate under certain implied inhibitions based on Pulitzer's own high moral hopes for American letters. Like a good many wealthy benefactors, he wanted to run things from the grave, and although the Pulitzer will specified, in the case of poetry, merely a "distinguished volume of verse"—there were no Verlaines or Oscar Wildes kicking around the country in 1911 to corrupt young readers—biography was to teach "patriotic and unselfish service to the people." In drama the criterion was to be "the educational value and power of the stage," and the winning novel called for presentation of "the wholesome atmosphere of American life and the highest standards of American manners and manhood." So solemnly were these strictures observed by the Advisory Board that in the early 1920's a minister was appointed a judge of fiction.

The taste buds of the reading public did not long endure this type of literary pablum, and in any case the Board's standards were soon relaxed in face of the onslaught of American realism. In 1929 the novel prize went to *Scarlet Sister Mary*, whose "seven illegitimate children," commented Professor Arthur Mizener, "can hardly have been the kind of thing Pulitzer had in mind when he urged 'the highest standards of American . . . manhood' on the judges' attention." The Advisory Board thereupon changed the rule to read "preferably one which shall best present the whole atmosphere of American life," and finally, in 1947, in a mood of final surrender, to "distinguished fiction . . . preferably dealing with American life."

In spite of this, novels that specialize in four-letter words, or overtly "frank" situations, have scant hope of getting through the various wickets that stand between nomination and prize. Nor do biographies of the rebellious or unpopular, as W. A. Swanberg discovered in 1961, when his *Citizen Hearst*, after being picked by the Pulitzer jury, ran afoul of the Trustees of Columbia University, who have the last word.

The real politics of Pulitzer winning takes place when the Advisory Board makes its final selections. They have, by this time, received the recommendations of the judges—four or five books in each category—and the horse trading begins in earnest. What makes the affair more complicated than most prize competitions is that the authors, whether they know it or not, are competing not only against each other but with a variety of journalists as well, and more than a few books have been scuttled by an editor who is also pushing another of his authors. To put the matter bluntly, he may have to sacrifice his most "distinguished" novel in order to put across his favorite foreign correspondent. The compromise candidate is often the winner. The 1952 choice in biography, for example, *Edmund Pendleton,* about an almost unheard-of statesman who died in 1803, was the result of some testy infighting on the Advisory Board. The book nominated lost a critical vote because one of the judges disliked the *employer* of the man who wrote it. To imply that such *ad hominem* arguments account for most Pulitzer choices

would be untruthful, but that they have played an important part there can be no question. Which may explain why so many Pulitzer books are the unexceptionable compromises that reflect rather than shape the popular taste.

The problems inherent in this prickly business have led to the suggestion that the government itself take on the job of determining literary excellence—after all, the Principality of Monaco shows no reluctance to do it—but the one serious attempt in this direction set official prize giving back fifty years. This occurred in 1948, when the financier Paul Mellon originally

Prizes for Poetry:

We Happy

Few

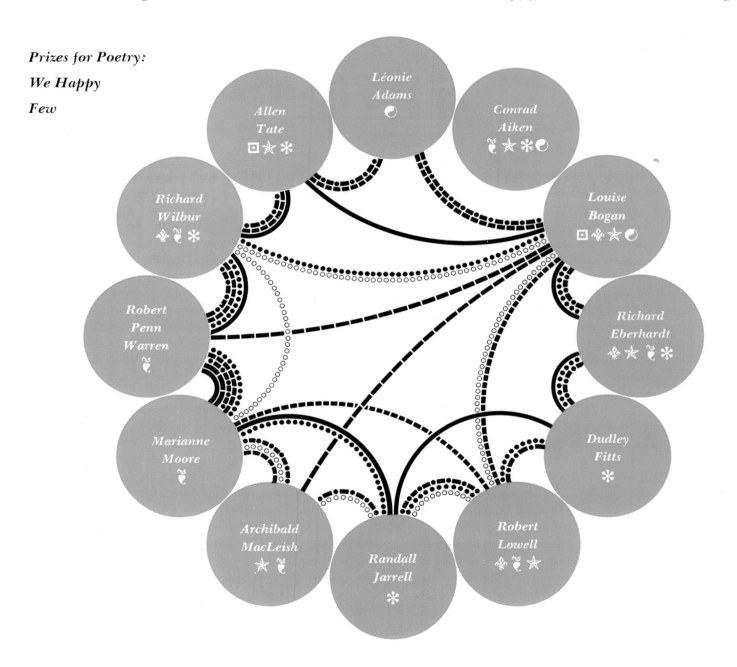

The Inner Twelve of American poetry is represented by this circle of poets, all (with one exception) involved as both givers and receivers of awards and distinctions. A line standing for each prize connects those who have been among the judges bestowing it; and for each (key at right) a symbol marks the recipients. A special prize should go to Conrad Aiken, who has managed to judge not while he was judged.

▪▪▪▪▪▪▪▪▪ **Brandeis University Creative Arts Award** ▣
▬▬▬▬▬▬ **Harriet Monroe Poetry Award** ⚜
▬▬▬▬▬▬ **Bollingen Prize in Poetry** ✩
•••••••••• **National Book Award in Poetry** ☙
▪•▪•▪•▪•▪ **National Institute of Arts and Letters Awards** ✳
ooooooooooo **Academy of American Poets** ☽

set up his Bollingen Prize in Poetry under the administration of the Library of Congress.

A jury of eminent "Fellows in American Letters" was appointed by the Library and instructed to bring in a sealed verdict. All went well until it was announced that the winner was an expatriate literary ne'er-do-well who had never so much as graced a dais and, worse yet, was crazier than most poets. Ezra Pound, in truth, was insane, and his only reason for being in the country at all was that his return had been arranged by the U.S. Army, which had arrested him in Italy for treason. Jacob Javits, then a representative in Congress, called for an investigation, which was not held; but the Joint House-Senate Library of Congress Committee lowered the boom anyway, and the Library withdrew its sponsorship. Just to be on the safe side, it also canceled existing prizes for prints and chamber music.

The irony of this tale is that Pound, who in his nearly forty-year career had always been recognized as one of our most talented poets, had never before received a prize, even when in his right mind. Unfortunately, he lacked an organized cheering section, and he was no politician.

A cynic might view the present quest for status-cum-prizes as a peculiarly American institution, comparable to the excesses of popular culture that have made us suspect abroad. Such is not the case. Prizemanship is world-wide, and exploding with the literacy rate. In Japan the annual Imperial Poetry Contest recently drew 7,491 entries, including one by Emperor Hirohito. In England, before it was discontinued a few years ago, the Guinness Prize for Poetry, worth $840, was underwritten by the well-known brewing company ("Guinness is good for you"), perhaps in mock protest against A. E. Housman's contention that "malt does more than Milton can/ To justify God's ways to man." Upwards of three thousand poems were submitted in an average year. As a nation of sophisticated readers, however, the British take their literary prizes in stride. There are not more than a dozen of importance, the oldest and most influential, the Hawthornden, dating back only to 1919. Also, this prize is unusual in being limited to authors under forty-one years of age. A roll call of winners constitutes a veritable Who's Who of literary celebrities—Graham Greene, Evelyn Waugh, Robert Graves, and Sean O'Casey are among them—but, in spite of this, winning the prize doesn't add much to a book's sale. Possibly the reading public has already discovered the author's talent. "The younger writer, when he does win [a prize]," comments one English critic, "is most likely to win it for the book after his first best seller."

It is on the Continent that awards are worth fighting for. In Spain, which is rampant with prizes—there are about twice as many as in the United States, some paying as much as $5,000 —almost every town of importance runs a competition, and the local writer is frequently second only to a matador in public esteem. This is fortunate. Because of economic conditions, it is impossible for all but a few writers to make a living out of the sale of books, and the only way to survive is by winning awards. These, happily, are supplied in quantity by academies, government agencies, publishing firms, municipalities and, in two cases, by restaurants. There are one hundred forty-six prizes all told, and it is accepted practice for an author to send his book to as many contests as possible. The most coveted is the Nadal, given for the best novel; it pays $2,600. The Premio Planeta, which is considered the runner-up, is worth $1,725. But it is not until a writer wins the government-sponsored Premio Cervantes de Literatura Hispanica that he has hit the jackpot. The Cervantes has a value of $5,000. All contests are obligingly held between November and May, thus avoiding the summer holiday season, when the Spanish stop reading books. Virtually all of the awards have come into existence during the Franco regime, and one need hardly add that in competing for them, being a good writer is not always as important as being a good Spaniard.

In Italy, too, literary passions run high, and the number of annual awards has now climbed to about a hundred. One of them is named after Hemingway, and another—the Balzan, worth a whopping $51,000—was awarded this year to an American, Samuel Eliot Morison. Germany does even better, with one hundred twenty-eight—one hundred eleven in the West German Republic. No more than forty have any real value, however, and most of these are administered by state or city governments, more or less in cultural competition with each other. However, in 1950 a number of German booksellers established a yearly prize of $2,500 for the writer, regardless of nationality, "who has made a contribution toward peace among men." It was won in 1957 by Thornton Wilder.

Oddly enough, the most celebrated German novel of the moment, Günter Grass's *The Tin Drum,** recently published in the United States, did not win a German prize. On the contrary, it won a French prize, the Prix du Meilleur Livre Etranger. In no other country in the world are the writer's chances of being honored better than in France. Here, literary recognition has become a national mania. The latest *Guide des Prix Littéraires*—an indispensable reference book for all aspiring French writers—lists four hundred seventy-five annual prizes. (The actual total, including awards given outside the country proper, is closer to a thousand.) Of these, five are of paramount importance, and among the five a pecking order has been established that ranks the Goncourt at the top, with the Femina, Renaudot, Médicis, and Interallié following in roughly that order.

In a sense, however, all French novel prizes are a protest against one another. The oldest and best known, the Goncourt, was established in the will of Edmond de Goncourt in 1884,

---

* See Gilbert Highet's book review in Horizon for March, 1963.

although the first of the awards was not made until 1903. Unlike Pulitzer, De Goncourt did not idealize the past which, for him, was represented by the hidebound French Academy. Therefore, he set up his own Academy. "My supreme wish, my wish which I beg young future academicians to hold always in their memory, is that the prize should be given to youth, to originality of talent, to bold new experiments of thought and form," he declared. By tradition, the Goncourt jury of ten critics makes its decision each year at Drouant's restaurant, over a meal of oysters and white wine. Since the judges are appointed for life, and soon drift into middle, and finally old age, "originality of talent" and "bold new experiments" ceased some time ago to be the hallmarks of a Goncourt novel.

The Prix Femina was set up in 1904. A jury of twelve women is appointed by two women's magazines—*Vie Heureuse* and *Revue Femina*—sensitive to the volatile fashions of the French reader. The Renaudot, on the other hand, is given to the books that, in the opinion of the jury, should have won the Goncourt or the Femina; its jury is composed exclusively of journalists. The Prix Médicis was established in 1957 under the newer and bolder influence of such "anti-novelists" as Alain Robbe-Grillet to ensure that at least one award each year would go to an avant-garde author. The winner of the Interallié, established in 1930 and limited to authors of "novels of international interest," shares his non-cash reward with the journalist jury—a celebration dinner.

n spite of the small amount of money distributed by most of these prize committees— the Goncourt award amounts to only $11.90—the ultimate stakes are high. Winning a Goncourt today means a sale of anywhere from 115,000 to 400,000 copies, with a minimum of $30,000 in royalties. The Renaudot and Femina are good for 80,000 copies. No wonder that the major French publishing houses shamelessly bombard members of the juries and the more influential critics. In a dispatch from Paris to the New York *Times* Douglas Cate once reported: "Every form of blandishment, inducement, persuasion and intimidation, short of open bribery, is used to sway decisions and to sew up votes in favor of this or that front running 'filly.' No lapel is left unfingered, no buttonhole ungripped, no influential chest untapped in a systematic campaign of social seduction that would have dumfounded a Dale Carnegie."

The author himself is expected to autograph a copy of his book for each juryman, and it is probably no coincidence that books from the House of Gallimard, six of whose authors are on the ten-man Goncourt jury, recently won six years in a row.

The results, from a strictly literary point of view, are seldom justified by these frenetic displays of immodesty. Few prize-winning French novels survive their season, and some of the more serious authors, among them Julien Gracq, refuse the prizes that are offered them. Gracq, for instance, in turning down the Goncourt, commented that "it was a hit or miss" competition. Others, who accept, later wish they hadn't. "It took me ten years to get over the Goncourt," declared Jean-Louis Bory, who won in 1945. "The readers that you try to reach, those of Gide and Claudel, do not read the Goncourt. They wouldn't touch it."

But those who do read the Goncourt—and the other prize winners—are in for some peculiar entertainment. A few years ago, the Prix Médicis was won by Henri Thomas with a novel, *John Perkins*. Thomas had previously taught at Brandeis University, and his picture of the United States, where the story is set, appealed strongly to the anti-Americanism that exists among certain elements of the French public. What made the novel unique, however, and in a sense increased its chances with the avant-garde jury, was its use of two different endings. In one, his American Perkins couple—"revolting, filthy," in the words of a Parisian critic—die dead drunk. In the other, they remain dead drunk but do not die.

This is not as queer as it sounds. French fiction, in its bid for attention from the judges, often pursues the bizarre. Here, briefly, are synopses of last year's principal winners:

In *Les Bagages de Sable* by Anna Langfus (Goncourt) a Polish refugee girl, living alone in Paris, goes off to the Côte d'Azur with an elderly Frenchman and becomes his mistress.

In Yves Berger's *Le Sud* (Femina) a young Frenchman is seduced by his sister, who wants to rescue him from their father's dream world of the nineteenth century. (Presumably the twentieth century is better.)

In *Le Veilleur de Nuit* by Simonne Jacquemard (Renaudot) an orphanage-bred young man living in the country conceals a girl for seventy-nine days in a Roman well in his garden.

Henri-François Rey's *Les Pianos Mécaniques* (Interallié) has been described by one critic as portraying "a society of promiscuous artistic and intellectual drunks" assembled on the Costa Brava.

La Baignoire by Colette Audry (Médicis) has for its heroine a female dog—a real bitch.

"It would be a mistake to think that the year-end prizes in France are a faithful reflection of the best in current literature," declared the critic Claude Mauriac not long ago.

The most coveted European award, as everybody knows, is the Nobel, in part because of its sizable monetary value (currently $40,000), but chiefly for the immense prestige it confers on the winner, who occasionally—as in the case of the Italian poet Salvatore Quasimodo—is lifted out of obscurity into international renown. Obscure or not, the writer who hopes for a Nobel had better be well-represented before the Swedish Academy.

This year, for example, eighty-one authors have been nominated; the type of campaign mounted in their behalf will play a not insignificant role in the final verdict. (The effort to put Quasimodo over was so successful that he was able to predict the outcome before the Academy's official announcement.) This

Among the Nobel Laureates Seldom Noted	*Among the Noted Who Never Won the Nobel*
GIOSUE CARDUCCI, Italy	IGNAZIO SILONE, Italy
PAUL VON HEYSE, Germany	MAXIM GORKY, Russia
VERNER VON HEIDENSTAM, Sweden	JAMES JOYCE, Ireland
KARL GJELLERUP, Denmark	ROBERT FROST, United States
HENRIK PONTOPPIDAN, Denmark	LEO TOLSTOY, Russia
CARL SPITTELER, Sweden	PAUL VALÉRY, France
LADISLAW STANISLAW REYMONT, Poland	MARCEL PROUST, France
GRAZIA DELEDDA, Italy	D. H. LAWRENCE, England
ERIK AXEL KARLFELDT, Sweden	THOMAS HARDY, England
FRANS EEMIL SILLANPÄÄ, Finland	JOSEPH CONRAD, England

may explain why French authors, backed by the aggressive French Academy, lead their colleagues in all other countries in the number of Nobels, although it should be added that aggressiveness alone does not guarantee success.

Although Alfred Nobel's will did not specify any special rotation of the prize, in a spirit of international good will the Committee has shown a fondness for distributing it over an unusually broad area. In a typical ten-year period, 1948–58, the literature prize went to England (thrice), the United States (twice), Sweden, France (twice), Iceland, Spain, and Russia. Russia didn't want it, and the author, Boris Pasternak, declined to attend the award ceremony (he did so, however, under circumstances which suggested that he was guiding himself by a prudent regard for the health and safety of those he loved). Italy, Finland, Ireland, and Germany have all been represented, and occasionally a Pole or Chilean will be honored; but by and large the important Nobel countries constitute a kind of European Common Market with strong ties to the United States. France, in this case too, has been the dominant partner.

One of the most concerted efforts in the history of the Prize was made in 1932, when a self-appointed group of Americans nominated Upton Sinclair. Before this extraordinary flanking attack came to an end, the Swedish Academy had heard from fifty-five countries, and had before it petitions containing seven hundred seventy signatures, including those of John Dewey, Albert Einstein, Bertrand Russell, Mrs. Thomas Hardy, and Bernard Shaw. The award that year went to John Galsworthy.

Conversely, the election of John Steinbeck in 1962 was achieved under almost phantom circumstances. Just who *did* nominate Steinbeck is something of a mystery. The American Academy of Arts and Letters—the most logical group—declined to do so; Steinbeck's publishers profess not to know; and the Swedish Academy isn't saying. However, the fact that the late Dag Hammarskjöld (a member of the Academy) was an ad-

mirer of Steinbeck's works undoubtedly did not hurt his chances.

Winning a prize does strange things to authors. In a burst of unpredictable generosity Shaw used his Nobel money to set up a fund for the translation of Swedish books into English. William Faulkner, who all his life had shunned the apparatus of literature, became panicky on the eve of his Nobel trip when he discovered that his rented dress suit had only one stripe down the trousers, where protocol called for two. (The trousers were hurriedly returned to the tailor for the addition of another stripe.) Like many Nobel winners, too, Faulkner went on to issue statements, and make junkets in behalf of the State Department. "Bill was never the same after he made the pilgrimage to Stockholm," declared an editor who knew him. "He even started writing letters to the New York *Times.*"

But the hazards go deeper than this, both for the author and for literature itself. From the reader's point of view prizes are seldom a reliable guide to the best that is being published in a country. In sixty years of Goncourts, only two outstanding novels—*Within a Budding Grove* and *Man's Fate*—have survived to become classics. Among the great writers of the twentieth century, Tolstoy, Paul Valéry, Stefan George, Gorky, Rilke, Croce, and Robert Frost failed to get the Nobel. In America F. Scott Fitzgerald never won any prize. Nor has Salinger. The bad boys, Dreiser and Farrell, were consistently ignored by the Pulitzer Committee, as were Thomas Wolfe and Dos Passos.

Perhaps this is not so bad. Hemingway once said that a writer gains in public stature after his work begins to deteriorate. The deterioration and the stature are not unrelated. There is a point at which men become so heaped-up with prizes that they can no longer be themselves: the award becomes a baited trap, forcing the writer to live up to an impossible public image. This can be destructive, as Hemingway himself discovered.

David Dempsey is a free-lance writer in the field of books and literature, and a former book columnist for the New York Times.

Equipages arrive within the gates of Vaux. But when King Louis came for a great fete in 1661, disaster followed.

NICOLAS FOUQUET

Fouquet dared to outdo his king by building France's greatest château, Vaux-le-Vicomte

The Minister's Fatal Showplace

By WILLIAM HARLAN HALE

...ouis overthrew him — and built Versailles

Young Louis XIV

o give a great party can be a dangerous thing. A few famous balls have become enshrined in history and golden legend—none more so than the Duchess of Richmond's in Brussels on the eve of Waterloo, remembered in the celebrated lines that begin, "There was a sound of revelry by night"—but there have been others whose immortality consists in the fact that their very splendor brought down disaster upon their givers.

The greater the party, sometimes, the greater the fall. In the severe depression winter of 1896–97 in New York, the Bradley Martins of high society threw a fabulous $300,000 ball in the newly completed Waldorf-Astoria Hotel, in the odd belief that the spreading of so much manna would alleviate the condition of the poor—and, when the Martins awoke next morning to find themselves called infamous, they sought permanent refuge in Europe. In the next decade another bemused and lordly New Yorker, the insurance heir James Hazen Hyde, staged an even costlier affair at Sherry's—a court soiree reproducing one of Louis XVI's, with authentic statuary, settings, costumes and liveries, imported for the occasion, along with the actress Réjane—but which also led to Hyde's long disappearance from his homeland, since his spending had helped trigger an investigation as to just what his Equitable Life Assurance Society was doing with its manna.

But perhaps the most self-destructive of all great parties was staged on August 17, 1661, by Nicolas Fouquet, the "Superintendent of Finances" of the France of young King Louis XIV, in order to show off his splendid new château of Vaux-le-Vicomte. The day dawned on a dazzling courtier at the peak of magnificence, with the King and the whole Court about to be his guests. It ended on a decision by Louis that was to strip Fouquet of both his office and his dream castle and to reduce him to disgrace and jail. The fete that misfired had another result: it caused Louis XIV, stricken with envy for his minister's pleasance, to build a greater Vaux-le-Vicomte of his own, and its name was Versailles.

Everyone who knew Fouquet knew that his feast would be very grand; but not even the King knew precisely how grand. In the outdoor theatre there was to be a new play, especially written by Molière, very much the talk of the Court and of the salons since the success of his satirical *Les Précieuses Ridicules* two seasons ago. Indoors, at dinner, France's leading composer, Lully, was to perform new music with his own orchestra. Dinner itself would be cooked and presented by the renowned Vatel. Among the nobles and Crown officials present with their ladies of fashion, the poet La Fontaine would be on hand to celebrate the occasion as its laureate: TEXT CONTINUED ON PAGE 80

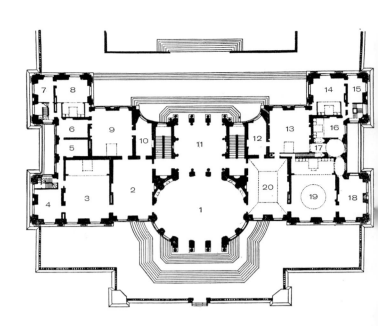

*S*een from its garden side (below), Vaux displays Le Nôtre's palatial landscaping, architect Le Vau's bold façade, and the artistic harmony achieved between both. The central mass is dominated by the cupola Le Vau raised over a two-story grand salon (see main-floor plan, with its original French designations, right) in a daring baroque departure from French style. Everything at Vaux was symmetrical and grand, though Le Vau did manage to squeeze a circular Cabinet des Bains (17) into his plan—another innovation, since few people then took baths. It was from atop the cupola that the final discharge of fireworks took place, climaxing Fouquet's great 1661 fete which inaugurated Vaux. His fall followed almost immediately.

Vaux's interiors were the province of the third and greatest of the brilliant trio Fouquet had assembled, the painter and designer Charles Le Brun, who richly decorated such rooms as the Chambre du Roi (above) which Louis XIV never slept in, and the Antichambre du Roi, now the château's library (below). A master of all arts and crafts, Le Brun also directed a whole army of cabinetmakers, tapestry weavers, metal smiths, and gilders on the site, and placed his classicist imprint on swirling statuary inside and out (right). One of the artists who worked on Vaux for Fouquet and Le Brun was a man whose fame was eventually to outshine theirs—Nicolas Poussin.

TEXT CONTINUED FROM PAGE 77

Le ciel en fut jaloux. Enfin, figure-toi
Que, lorsqu'on eut tiré les toiles
Tout combattit à Vaux pour le plaisir du Roi,
La musique, les eaux, les lustres, les étoiles.

And there was to be more: perhaps too much more.

The start of the festivities at Vaux, some fifty kilometers southeast of Paris, had been announced for six o'clock, in order to give time for the spectacles and diversions planned by Fouquet to last far into the summer night. If the King was not to delay them, he would have to set out in mid-afternoon from his own château of Fontainebleau thirty kilometers southward, for three hours of coaching across the hills and valleys of the Ile de France in blistering August heat. But young Louis, only twenty-three this summer, had already acquired those habits of punctuality, punctilio, and consideration (to those who merited his consideration) that were to mark his immensely long reign, and his Court was in its carriages, in its perukes and thick lace, promptly at three in order to arrive at M. Fouquet's on time, heat or not.

Accompanied by a troop of Gardes-françaises and musketeers and the usual outriders and pages, the cortege included such august personages as the Queen Mother; Louis's younger brother, Prince Philippe (in French court parlance, simply "Monsieur"); Philippe's recent bride, Princess Henrietta of England, with whom the King was presently romancing ("Madame"); the ranking Prince de Condé ("M. le Prince"); the dukes of Bourbon, Beaufort, Guise, and many others—an extraordinary turnout to be journeying all this distance to the country seat of a man born a commoner. Yet of all the personages of France, there was none who held higher claim to the King's consideration than Nicolas Fouquet, the Anjou lawyer's son who had risen by soaring ambition and extraordinary dexterity to become *vicomte de Melun et de Vaux, ministre d'Etat, surintendant des finances, et procureur général,* a brilliant patron of the arts, the glass of fashion and, since the death of Cardinal Mazarin just three months ago, the most powerful man in France after Louis himself.

The long cavalcade wound on until at length, approaching a high ground, it caught sight of the immense new pleasure dome of the King's favorite. Surmounted by its cupola and gilded lantern, the château of white stone still lay at a middle distance, centered in a vast panorama that extended almost as far as the eye could reach. On either side were rolling woods; but a superb swath had been cut through them, dipping gently from the highway into a river vale and bringing up at the far slope, so that on descending toward the gates one could take in the whole prospect at once—yet in three acts, so to speak.

Nearest, behind a curtain of grilles and a line of heroic sculptured standards that stood like heralds to announce the enclosure, there spread a stately forecourt (see pages 76–77) divided into rectilinear avenues and planted squares, with matching outbuildings and copses on either side and a moat beyond: that could be called Act One, the preparation—a composition of perfect though severe symmetry. Just beyond the moat was Act Two, the dramatic unfolding—the great house of Vaux-le-Vicomte itself, massive but exuberant, rising in a proud profusion of balustrades, classical orders, pediments,

oeils-de-boeuf, and mansards to a forest of statuary on the eaves and roof tops. Finally, beyond this, the eye could proceed to Act Three, the joyous resolution—Vaux's sparkling and playful gardens with their arabesques, sculptured nymphs, pools, lovers' groves, grottoes, fountains (some fifty in number), and *jets d'eau* (some two hundred) culminating in a grand cascade.

The King was received at the gates by a host twice his age, not equal to him in physical stature, dark-eyed, slight, and compact in contrast to Louis's tall, blue-eyed majesty, yet of a nimbleness and verve of bearing that belied his years and made him seem a worthy peer of so young a king, especially since the latter had grown so very stately when so very young. The radiant host, M. Fouquet, handed down his royal guests from their coaches. First they were shown the outdoor sights, the King being particularly taken with the waterworks, which he pronounced finer than anything at Tivoli or Frascati—without having to add that they were far, far finer than his own at Fontainebleau, since everyone knew that he had little more there than a lake. The gardens as a whole were beyond compare: they had been laid out by the brilliant André Le Nôtre, whom the Crown had first employed to design the Tuileries gardens of the Louvre, but whom Fouquet had since taken into his own service to design something much greater.

Fouquet could point out garden statuary by numerous prominent artists, especially Nicolas Poussin, while ranks of admiring courtiers lined the walks as the King passed between them. (*"Ces courtisans chargés de rubans et de plumes faisaient le plus bel aspect que l'on puisse imaginer,"* one account of the festivity states; *"et c'était une confusion de si belles choses qu'on ne peut l'exprimer."*) Then the King, returning from the fountains, viewed the second, or garden-side, façade of the château—more striking even than the first (see panorama, pages 78–79). Here its architect, Louis Le Vau, who had first made his mark with some pavilions for Cardinal Mazarin's château at Vincennes, had outdone himself with a spectacular oval protuberance and dome, breaking all traditions of French château design and infusing new Italian ideas of grandeur into it.

Château indeed! With its magnificence of elevation (its dominating dome rose almost sixty feet above a two-story grand salon of regal width), and with its tiers of grand apartments sweeping out into four tall corners, this was beyond anything yet built in the French countryside by anyone less than a king. Blois, Chenonceaux, Chambord themselves paled beside it, while Louis's own favorite retreat of Fontainebleau was an aged rabbit warren of building and rebuilding, and his late father's hunting lodge at Versailles was still no more than—a hunting lodge.

But Vaux-le-Vicomte's richest splendors remained to be revealed to the King when Fouquet led him through its apartments, some still unfinished in the minister's rush to exhibit the whole establishment without delay. Flanking the Grand Salon—with its pilasters, clerestory lights, caryatid statues, and overhead vault—ran a riot of rooms decked out with tapestries, friezes, garlands, festoons, medallions, cartouches, gilt moldings, shimmering chandeliers and, above all, with swirling murals and ceiling frescoes that represented most of the classical pantheon, each figure chosen with allegorical point.

80

Thus in the Chambre du Roi (one of a suite of three of his finest rooms that Fouquet had decorated for royal use—see page 79) Jupiter, Mars, Mercury, and Bacchus were depicted on the four walls, evidently with intent to allude to four qualities of the King and his reign: power, valor, vigilance, and abundance, respectively. The lofty Salon des Muses displayed all the Muses, two by two, and also a complex ceiling allegory, "The Triumph of Fidelity," which was to be read as a reminder of Fouquet's loyalty to the King during the recent uprising of nobles called the *Fronde*. But the most triumphant ceiling painting was that in the Salon d'Hercule, which showed the classic hero borne aloft and seated on Olympus beside Jupiter, Diana, and Juno. Who in this instance was Hercules meant to symbolize? To anyone who knew Fouquet, and particularly the motto he had chosen for his armorial bearings, *Quo non ascendam?* ("How high can't I rise?"), the answer was readily at hand: Hercules was Fouquet himself.

The King gazed upward and took all this in, as he did the emblem of a cursive F that appeared over and over again in the scrollwork of the salons, very much as the royal initial L had appeared above doorways designed for his own kingly predecessors in the Louvre.* All these paintings and decorations, Louis learned from his host, were due to the third of the trio of extraordinary talents Fouquet had assembled to create Vaux-le-Vicomte—Charles Le Brun, precocious painter, sculptor, master organizer of all arts and crafts; not yet forty, and in command of the thousand-odd artisans who had been working on Vaux, including a whole tapestry factory especially set up in the adjoining village of Maincy.

The diners—there may have been something like five hundred —sat down to Vatel's feast of ortolans, pheasants, quail, partridge, and assorted bisques and ragouts, accompanied by a long list of wines. Lully performed with twenty-four violins supported by other instruments. At one point King Louis admired the dinner service: "What admirable plate."

"Pardon, Sire, it is not plate, it is gold."

The King, reportedly: "We have nothing like this at the Louvre."

Seated not far from him, Mme de La Fayette observed his demeanor amid so much magnificence, and later recalled, "The King was astonished, and Fouquet became aware that he was astonished." Did Fouquet at this moment realize the peril he was courting in daring to outshine his king? But there was no stopping now; the show must go on to its grand finale.

After dinner everyone went outdoors again, and to the open-air theatre. Three knocks sounded. Dark-visaged Molière himself appeared before the footlights, in everyday clothes, putting on the air of a man surprised by this command performance— and indeed he had written and produced in just fifteen days a new masque comedy, *Les Fâcheux* (*The Nuisances*), in which he

* Sometimes, engagingly, Fouquet's F was combined at Vaux with the representation of a squirrel, suggesting that Fouquet had seen an affinity between himself and that quick, vertiginous animal, so deft at supplying its own nest. Whether or not he was playing upon this thought, he was no doubt playing upon the word, since "squirrel," though *écureuil* in French, was also *fouquet* in the old Angevin dialect of the province in which he had been raised.

*L*e Brun (top) was so precocious that he won his first painting commission from Richelieu at fifteen. Employed to celebrate Fouquet's glory, he covered Vaux's ceilings with such allegorical showpieces as "The Triumph of Truth" (above). King Louis himself, though, was just as avid for this sort of grandiose self-celebration and took over Le Brun as premier peintre du Roi, having him execute such stupefying designs as those in Versailles's Galerie des Glaces (below).

was also to play the leading part. After apologizing to his royal guests for his inadequacy, he withdrew to change into costume while a lengthy prologue was delivered, as written for the occasion by another poet in Fouquet's service, Paul Pellisson.

Pour voir en ces beaux lieux le plus grand Roi du monde,
Mortels, je viens à vous de ma grotte profonde . . .

So Pellisson's rhymed obeisance to His Majesty began, followed by the entrance of "numerous dryads, accompanied by fauns and satyrs" from among the surrounding trees and sculptures, to perform a dance as a still further introduction to the play (not by any means one of Molière's best). After three acts and a concluding ballet, at about midnight, came Fouquet's final surprise—an explosion of fireworks such as had never been seen before in France. Hundreds of lanterns had already been lit in Vaux's gardens. Now the Italian Torelli, a master of illuminations, lit up the sky itself with a cascade of rockets of every color, including a blaze of fleurs-de-lis in sparkling white, and then topped even this effect by a smashing discharge of Roman candles from the lantern of Vaux, accompanied by a blast of cannon and a salute of trumpets.

It was distinctly overdone. The King, a master already at covering his displeasure with sovereign correctness, remained briefly for the late-evening supper that followed, but then, disdaining to stay the night in the royal suite prepared for him, coached home with his Court to Fontainebleau, sleeping all the way, we are told, and arriving there about dawn.

It may have been a fitful sleep, for he had a stern resolve to make. He had been concerned for several months at the way his *surintendant* was managing the realm's finances, even though the late Mazarin and many others had conceded that this delightful courtier was a financial wizard. Why was it that the royal treasury remained so bare while Fouquet's own had become so ample? Tonight's spectacle could only confirm the suspicions which Fouquet's enemies, headed by the austere, rising Jean-Baptiste Colbert, had tried to implant in the King's mind: the moment had come to bring down a man who had grown too great.

So, within three weeks, after more evidence had been gathered against him, Fouquet was arrested at Nantes in Brittany by royal warrant on a charge of embezzlement. Vaux-le-Vicomte and his other estates were seized. A long trial followed, resulting in his conviction and the forfeiture of all his property. Meanwhile Louis had determined to show a splendor of his own (with financial assistance from Colbert, who now took over the royal treasury), and set out to build Versailles as a far greater Vaux—the men in charge of the work being none other than Fouquet's own team of Le Brun, Le Vau, and Le Nôtre. Molière, too, passed into the King's service, staging indoor and outdoor theatricals at Versailles after the style at Vaux; so did Vatel, with his dinners; so did Torelli, with his fireworks. In fact, the King was so anxious to turn to his own use all that was best at Vaux that he even had many of its statues transported to his new palace, along with some 1,250 shrubs and trees lately planted in the gardens of the fallen Fouquet.

How could so gifted a man as Nicolas Fouquet, veteran of thirty years' office-holding and of a lifetime's knowledge of Europe's most tortuous court, have set his course for such total disaster? His great miscalculation was not that he mismanaged the King's money but that he misread his mind. Moreover, he had misread the dates on the calendar of Louis's evolution. Until March 8, 1661, Louis was still in the eyes of those around him a stylish but unproven and tame young monarch, captive to the magisterial Mazarin, who had been the lad's preceptor ever since Louis had ascended to the throne at the age of four. Queen Mother Anne of Austria, rid of her feeble and loveless husband Louis XIII, had let Mazarin become her favorite, presumably her lover, and virtual regent of the realm. But on March 9, the very day after Mazarin died, Louis announced that henceforth he would be his own chief minister, obviously glad in his turn to be rid of the presumptuous and avaricious cleric who had oppressed all the years of his youth.

Therewith began Louis XIV's assumption of personal, absolute rule—a regime which over the decades was to prove splendid for France but which in just a few months was to be fatal to Fouquet, the dashing courtier closest to the throne and so dazzled by the hope of becoming the next Mazarin that he failed to realize a virile, pent-up monarch grown into his majority might wish to be every inch a king and brook no rivals.

Fouquet knew much, but was blinded with overweening *hubris*. He knew that Louis particularly resented the great landed nobles who during his youth had staged uprisings against royal authority—an outbreak that at one point had led Paris rioters to invade his very bedroom in the Louvre. The King had plans to put these *Frondeurs* into their place at last; moreover, he was bent on removing his seat of rule from Paris, in order never again to expose himself to such humiliations as he had experienced there, and to make his palace in the countryside the center to which all nobles and placemen must come to bend the knee. Yet now Fouquet himself had built at Vaux the greatest country palace in France—and, as if that were not enough, he had also acquired an island stronghold on the Breton coast, Belle-Isle, which he had proceeded to fortify.

The building of great estates that would reflect new wealth and show off new architecture was then very much the rage in France. The late Cardinal Richelieu had built grandly for himself at Rueil and in Poitou; Mazarin, at Vincennes. Claude de Bullion had a splendid new showplace at Wideville, also by Le Vau; the Comte de Servien, another at Meudon, complete with colossal terraces and grottoes. But Fouquet, fabulously wealthy from his take as *surintendant*, bought and built like a man obsessed. He had acquired two great mansions in Paris; the country seat of Saint-Mandé, not far from Mazarin's own; the seigniory of Maincy, where he would build Vaux; and a number of lesser domains—all this before he went on to Belle-Isle and the completion of the château that was to be his apotheosis or, as he put it to his judges when on trial, "*mon établissement principal . . . où je voulois laisser quelques marques de l'éstat où j'avois esté.*"

Fouquet was rash, vainglorious, and corrupt. Colbert claimed that only one half of the immense tax revenues Fouquet was charged with collecting for the King ever got into the King's hands; and while this was a jealous rival's exaggeration (the state's total revenues from the *taille* (a personal tax), the salt tax, and other imposts and duties then ran to some 140 million livres a year), unquestionably many millions were diverted each year into Fouquet's own pocket. Vaux alone may have cost him more than a million—perhaps the equivalent of $10 million today.

He was also, when he came to build and to patronize the arts, in general a man of superlative taste. Perhaps he was the embodiment of many talents in disarray in a France where new talents could rise quickly. Success dawned early for him: son of a provincial family of legal distinction (what the French called the *noblesse de robe*), he was only sixteen when his father's friend Richelieu gave him his first diplomatic assignment. At twenty-one, as *Maître de Requêtes,* he was a judicial officer of the kingdom; at twenty-seven, the inspector of its armies of the North; and at thirty-eight, under Mazarin's patronage, the *surintendant* who was to rise to such heights and then to such a fall. Two brilliant marriages had established his wealth; then came those dazzling years when as head of the King's treasury he was responsible to no one for his accounts save the King himself, with the result that he mixed up Louis's and his own.

Yet, while making out false returns and signing away his nation's future tax receipts, he lived a many-sided, exuberant life in the arts, patronizing the literary salons of Mlle de Scudéry and Mme du Plessis-Bellière; writing verses of his own; gathering around him and subsidizing a coterie of young spirits ranging from the poets La Fontaine, Scarron, and Pellisson to the playwrights Molière and Corneille; installing in his great house of Saint-Mandé a library of 30,000 volumes ranging from architecture to mathematics; buying Bellinis, Breughels, Veroneses; and finally, at Vaux, assembling the unique team of Le Vau, Le Nôtre, and Le Brun, who made a classic unity of his miscellany of dreams.

The shrewd King had spotted the perfection of Fouquet's taste no less than the man's excess. But in jealously copying and enlarging that taste at Versailles, he doubled and redoubled the excess, with the result that his new palace got quite out of scale, even for a glorious king. Le Vau designed for him façades that went on too long; Le Brun, now *premier peintre du Roi,* covered endless interiors with allegorical scenes that were too many and too alike and that palled courtiers then as they do visitors now; and Le Nôtre, ordered to design gardens several times the size of Vaux's, produced those forbidding vistas that, as Saint-Simon remarked, "one admired but avoided."

Versailles was Louis's vengeful triumph—an assertion of majesty over Fouquet, over the nobles of France, and over the people of Paris, from whom he had now removed himself into the most haughty isolation. Yet the King's new palace lacked a quality that Fouquet's short-lived one had, ill-advised as it was: exuberance. Versailles was stupendous but dull.

In its series on unique palaces HORIZON *has discussed the Grand Seraglio (May, 1959), the castles of Bavaria's King Ludwig II. (January, 1961), Blenheim (September, 1961), the Brighton Pavilion (November, 1962), and Hadrian's Villa (May, 1963).*

S

oon after he left Vaux between these gates, the envious King Louis set about building Versailles, using Fouquet's artists Le Brun, Le Vau, and Le Nôtre, and much of its fallen owner's property as well. Did he, in turn, build too grandly— as his minister Fouquet had done before him? Many have thought so. Vaux itself was left to a desultory history: returned in a denuded state to the disgraced Fouquet's family, it was bought by a French marshal in 1705, escaped demolition during the French Revolution, deteriorated, and finally came into the hands of another private French owner who set out to restore what was left.

N.Y.; CULVER; 3: CULVER 2: VANDAMM, 3: CULVER

The most disconcerting thing about Orson Welles's screen version of *The Trial* is that in retrospect it doesn't seem to matter. At the moment, it is entertaining; at times its ingenuity and insight are admirable; it commits (except for a grotesquely inappropriate final shot) no factual offense against Kafka's novel. Yet a few days after I had seen it, it had slipped off my mind and left the book just as it was.

The same thing, I find, can be said of the pictures Welles made of *Macbeth* and *Othello*. They had great cinematic vigor, they were clearly intended as shocks to entrenched attitudes toward both the plays themselves and the suitability of the screen for the transmission of Shakespeare. But whereas I have had to work at erasing Olivier's movie-Hamlet from memory, Welles's Macbeth and Othello have obligingly bleached away.

How does it happen that someone of Welles's stature in the theatre can work to such impermanent ends? And, if I am right in this, how does it happen that he continues to be a figure of international fascination? The answer may lie in the fact that Welles is a quite unusual species of man—he is an adult prodigy. And to explain what that implies I must digress a bit.

A child prodigy, and Orson Welles was almost the archetype, differs from a child in that he never plays with things—he *uses* them. Give him a typewriter and he will publish a newspaper, give him an easel and he will paint your portrait, give him blocks and he will design a model city, give him a gun—no, don't give him a gun. Some children display specific talents—for music, mathematics, poker; the true child prodigy is born with the gift for instant accomplishment.

Welles, for example, was staging his own adaptations of Shakespeare (he had been given a model theatre) before he could read. And he taught himself to read at the age of three by using *A Midsummer Night's Dream* as a primer. At ten, when he was examined by a group of psychologists assembled in Madison, Wisconsin, he was described in the local paper as a poet, painter, cartoonist, and actor; the reporter did not know, apparently, that he was also a pianist, an accomplished magician, and a critic of Nietzsche. At that meeting, by the way, he routed the brain probers by replying to their questions with erudite pronouncements of complete irrelevance. In short, instant accomplishment.

The prognosis for children who show this gift for handling the adult world as though it were their rattle is statistically not very promising. The child of single and singular talent often develops into a talented adult; the way is much harder for the generally prodigious child. A few become excellent men and women, but in more cases they are eventually overtaken by their contemporaries and find themselves ill-prepared to compete on equal terms. It is only rarely that the child prodigy converts into an adult prodigy.

After adolescence the difference between the prodigy and the talented is not so easily defined. The most reliable guide, perhaps, is that in the former case public attention tends to focus more on the remarkable circumstances surrounding an accomplishment than on the accomplishment itself. And it can therefore happen that the prodigy's reputation is not integrally associated with his achievements.

ADULT PRODIGY

By ROBERT HATCH

Orson Welles was a leading man at 18,

scared the radio audience silly at 23,

infuriated the Hearst empire at 25,

and is still a baggy trickster at 48.

What will he do when he grows up?

Looming over the harbor of Macao, Welles puffs placidly on a stogie after completing a recent suspense movie called *Ferry to Hong Kong*.

The Boy: aged three, when a composer dedicated a musical suite to him

The Juvenile Lead: at 18, about to set off on a road tour with Katherine Cornell

The Voice: at 22, working as a radio actor for CBS

If it is good luck to be Orson Welles—and I think it must be one of the most exciting experiences a man could have—then Welles has been lucky all his life. He was born in 1915 in Kenosha, Wisconsin, which is on Lake Michigan. As a child, he was surrounded by precisely the sort of adults a prodigy should cultivate. His mother, Beatrice Ives, a beauty and a concert pianist, introduced him to artistic society in Chicago when he was little more than a baby. Like most prodigies, he was much in the company of grownups, and he attributes his disconcerting knack of being able to carry on one conversation while absorbing two or three others going on in his vicinity to the early habit of eavesdropping at the vivacious gatherings he attended with his mother.

She died when the boy was nine, and he returned to his father (the parents had separated), a retired manufacturer and inventor—an improved bicycle lamp, a mess kit used by the U.S. Army in World War I—who was to devote the rest of his life to travel and good living. He was named Richard H. Welles, and a race horse, as well as a restaurant and a cigar, was named after him. Young Welles had seen Europe and the Far East by the time he was in his early teens; he had become accustomed to champagne suppers and the laughter of beautiful women.

Then there was Dr. Maurice Bernstein, who visited the family professionally, and who guessed that Welles was a prodigy at the age of one and a half. It was Dr. Bernstein who provided the model theatre, the paints and brushes, the magic kit, which the child seized with infallible hands. It was Dr. Bernstein who, as legal guardian of the teen-ager when he became an orphan, allowed Welles to declare Harvard superfluous and to go off instead on a sketching jaunt through Ireland, which

within a year had brought him to Dublin and to leading parts in the repertory of the Gate Theatre.

Welles was not uneducated; he spent five years, from eleven to fifteen, in school. Again he was lucky, for the Todd School of Woodstock, Illinois, was very possibly the only educational institution in the country that would have tolerated Welles or that Welles would have tolerated himself. Roger Hill, the headmaster, was undismayed on being told that Welles was devoting his energies in history to exposing the ignorance of the eminent Egyptologist, James H. Breasted; and he was able to adjust the curriculum so that his unusually energetic student could produce, direct, and act in an average of eight plays per school year. Todd has ever since rather specialized in dramatics, and Welles has maintained an interest in his only alma mater.

After the season at the Gate, which Welles got by telling Hilton Edwards, its director, a wholly preposterous and little credited yarn of stellar performances at the Theatre Guild, he returned to New York, aged seventeen, and was offended by the city's failure to take any formal notice of his presence. He thereupon retired to Morocco where, as the guest of a local prince, he worked on a school edition of Shakespeare which he and Roger Hill brought out together and which has sold one hundred thousand copies over the years.

On his next trip home he met Thornton Wilder, who sent him to Alexander Woollcott, who introduced him to Katherine Cornell, who engaged him as a juvenile for a repertory tour on which she was then starting. He was eighteen, and we may say that his status as a child prodigy was over.

Welles's career now begins to accelerate, and no attempt will be made to touch on every event.

Holy Terror: at 23, when he threw millions into a panic with his straight-faced radio production of H. G. Wells's *The War of the Worlds*

Family Fellow: Welles with his first wife, Virginia Nicholson, and daughter Christopher in 1938. His most celebrated helpmeet: Rita Hayworth

Stubble-maker: training a beard for *Heart of Darkness,* a movie never made

Newly Mustached: reading a script, New York, late 1940's

Straw Hatter: directing a breakneck farce, *Too Much Johnson,* at a summer theatre in 1938

Movie Man: in 1940 Welles, in tribal costume, having reached Hollywood with his Mercury Players

In the mid-thirties, the country was still far down in the Depression; as a time for launching oneself in the theatre it had only one thing to recommend it—relatively few vessels were being launched and you could make a relatively big splash. In 1935 Welles was offered the lead in *Panic*, an experimental verse play by Archibald MacLeish which derived its title from the Wall Street collapse of 1933 and in which the banker (Welles) was named McGolferty. This in itself was not much of a splash; the play was scheduled for only three performances, with the critics invited, prudently, on the second night. But John Houseman was a member of the sponsoring group, and he and Welles were soon to become a memorable theatre team. In 1936 the Federal Theatre Project (WPA) engaged them to produce an all-Negro *Macbeth* in Harlem (it was set in Haiti and employed witch doctors instead of witches). In addition to its dubious artistic premise, this enterprise involved some very tricky racial diplomacy. Welles survived both the events on stage and the agitation along 125th Street, and went on to direct for the WPA a production of *Dr. Faustus* that was presented on a bare stage and organized by the use of great sheets of light beamed from banks of overhead spots.

He then set to work on Marc Blitzstein's *The Cradle Will Rock,* and at that point the WPA panicked. It smelled subversion in the script and locked the theatre. Welles and Houseman found another theatre and on their own opened *The Cradle Will Rock* without scenery or costumes and with Blitzstein himself at the piano. That was the beginning of The Mercury Theatre which, in the next two years, 1937–1938, produced the famous anti-Fascist *Julius Caesar* (Welles played Brutus in a shabby overcoat and a slouch hat); *The Shoemaker's Holiday,*

Welles the Actor: six feet three inches tall, with a round face and high fore-head, a "trademark" voice of incomparable resonance, a defiant stance, and a certain total presence un-mistakably his, Welles should be physically limited in his roles, and thus a prime candidate for type-casting. But his mastery of disguises and fa-cial contortions gives his acting a sheer range and bravura unexcelled on the stage and screen today, as can be seen from the photographs that follow in chronological sequence.

Grim: Captain Shotover in Shaw's play *Heartbreak House,* 1938

Honorable: Brutus in the modern-dress *Julius Caesar,* 1937

an Elizabethan romp by Thomas Dekker that galloped irresistibly through a set composed entirely of unpainted lath latticework; and Shaw's *Heartbreak House,* in which Welles, now twenty-three, played the octogenarian Captain Shotover. It is perhaps the most unplayable of Shaw's works, but it was seen to foretell the fall of England's house, which made it a tract for the times.

Those plays, in those money-tight days, were not profitable, but by 1938 Welles was a veteran radio actor. He played innumerable real-life public figures for "The March of Time"; he was "The Shadow"; he was hired for so many dramatic programs that he sometimes arrived in the studio as the show was going on the air and grabbed a script with no advance notion of whether he was playing hero, villain, or idiot bystander. There were times when he hired an ambulance to get himself rapidly through the midtown traffic; it was an expense he could well afford, since his fees were running to $17,000 a year. Much of that money went to support the Mercury.

We come now to 8 P.M. on the evening of October 30, 1938 (Halloween), when The Mercury Theatre of the Air, directed by and starring Orson Welles, was to give its regular weekly entertainment in the series called "First Person Singular." The idea was to adapt famous stories—*Jane Eyre, Treasure Island, Oliver Twist, The 39 Steps,* were some that had been used—to a formula peculiarly suitable to radio. As Welles explained it: "When someone comes on the air and says 'This happened to me,' you've got to listen." They certainly listened to the offering of October 30th, *The War of the Worlds* by H. G. Wells.

The narrative method used on this particular evening was as

Visitor: not Mao Tse-tung but Welles, talking business (with producer Alexander Korda)

Connoisseur: "It is impossible," Welles has said, "to pay too much attention to good food or to a beautiful wo-man." At Macao, in 1959

ebrity: Welles in is in 1950, scribbling ographs for the fans

Exuberant: the middle-aged, power-mad publisher *Citizen Kane,* 1941

Domineering: with false skull as senile Kane, 1941

Sinister: Colonel Haki in *Journey into Fear,* 1942

Debonair: "Orson the Magnificent" in a conjuring act from *Follow the Boys,* 1943

Romantic: Rochester in *Jane Eyre,* 1944

Paternal: with six-year-old Natalie Wood in *Tomorrow Is Forever,* 1945

simple as it proved devastating. Welles created a fake newscast (a form of entertainment subsequently avoided by all the networks). He updated the original story to the night in question and set its critical episode in Grovers Mill, New Jersey, a remote town that was yet not far from New York, and within easy reach of a very large segment of the listening audience. After the customary station introduction and a brief "foreword" by Welles, both of which made it crystal-clear that this was fiction and both of which were as clearly missed by millions of late tuners, the "show" started with a weather forecast, followed by dance music from the Hotel Park Plaza (there was no such hotel) in New York. There came shortly an interruption: Intercontinental Radio News (no such agency) had just issued a bulletin about several large explosions on Mars that had been detected on the earth a half-hour earlier. Then more music, then additional explosion details, followed by a "background" interview with Professor Pierson (Welles) of the Princeton observatory. This was in turn interrupted by a flash: "a huge flaming object" had fallen in a farmer's field near Grovers Mill.

No one should have been fooled. There was the standard station opening, there was a mid-hour identification, and no other station on the air was "reacting" to the ghastly events. Further, the events took place at ludicrous speeds. (For example, Dr. Pierson would have had to drive from Princeton to Grovers Mill over the back roads of New Jersey at several hundred miles an hour to arrive at the moment when he was heard to say, from observations made at a distance of some thirty yards, that "the metal casing is definitely extraterrestrial.") Finally, one would have thought that a "meteor" with

a screw top was a sufficiently trite hobgoblin to disabuse the most gullible. One would have thought wrong.

America, or a significant segment of America, panicked as Welles spun the old Martian thriller out over the CBS network. The worst disorders occurred in New Jersey, near the place where "the monsters had landed." Highways were blocked with refugees fleeing the lethal gas of the invading octopi; the telephone system broke down, police stations were jammed, and at least one of them advised hysterical questioners to follow precisely the advice coming from their radios. It all lasted only an hour or so, but the anguish induced across the whole country is entirely incalculable.

I am not going to discuss the reasons for this extraordinary response to a yarn so shopworn that Welles had hesitated to use it. The incident is analyzed in detail in Hadley Cantril's sociological study, *The Invasion from Mars.* In defense of the common sense of the American public (and it is hardly a sufficient defense), it should be recalled that the capitulation of Chamberlain at Munich had occurred only a month earlier, and terror was epidemic in the world.

The relevant point is that, as a prodigy, Welles was lucky again. He hadn't meant to cause suffering with his Halloween charade; he hadn't schemed to become a national focus of mixed admiration and anger. Nevertheless, events had shown in the most dramatic way conceivable that the touch of Welles was unlike the touch of other men.

And the proof continued to pile up. Hollywood signed him to one of the richest, most open contracts ever offered a newcomer (that and a beard grown for a production of *The Heart of Darkness,* which he never made, earned Welles the instant

1–6: CULVER; 7–8: GEORGE KARGER, PIX INC.; 9–12: CULVER

sipated: one of many
~~les~~ parts in
stage show *Around the*
~~rld in 80 Days,~~ 1946

Inscrutable: a contrasting
role in the same play

Touching: nose to nose
with Rita Hayworth in *The
Lady from Shanghai,* 1948

Ambitious: Macbeth
in Shakespeare's tragedy,
1948

Furtive: Cagliostro in
Black Magic, 1949

Dangerous: Cesare
Borgia in *Prince of
Foxes,* 1949

and virulent hatred of the film colony). His first big picture was *Citizen Kane;* it is the best picture he has ever made and probably the most notorious picture ever made in America.

We may safely ignore the disclaimers—*Citizen Kane* was based on the life of William Randolph Hearst. It held that life up to scorn and pity; worse, it envisioned its end, and Hearst, who had a morbid fear of death, trained the fire of the most powerful and ruthless newspaper empire in America on Welles, on RKO, on Hollywood. There was no battle—RKO made a few bold statements, Hedda Hopper fired some girlish grapeshot at Hearst's Louella Parsons, Welles tried quite futilely to get hold of his creation. RKO, and certainly Hollywood, had no intention of fighting for anything as abstract as a principle. To this day *Citizen Kane* has never had a wide circulation. One of Welles's holds on fame, then, is that he made a great picture which has had fewer viewers than any of similar renown.

Citizen Kane opens with a fake "March of Time" newsreel on the death of "the great man" that is as brilliant as the Martian broadcast. At its conclusion the lights come up on what is seen to be a preview studio, where the editor is heard expressing dissatisfaction because the picture does not get to the central "truth" about Kane.

This is not entirely likely—it being no function of newsreels to provide pinpoint analysis—but it does provide a splendid narrative device. A reporter is assigned to track down the meaning of Kane's last word—"Rosebud"—and the film proper is a series of flashbacks showing the public and private Kane as he is remembered by the men and women who were closest to him. These portraits are alike—but not quite; and the real portrait is the sum of the discrepancies.

What makes *Citizen Kane* so good is not the rather thin psychological thread that ends in "Rosebud." It is rather that Welles drew a character of genuine stature, and by the reporting device, showed his man with depth, clarity, anger, understanding, and compassion. Welles was superb in the role of Kane. I doubt that there is much autobiography in the characterization—at least conscious autobiography, though Welles did name Kane's lifelong friend and adviser after Dr. Bernstein. But Kane also was more prodigy than giant, and Welles understood his subject. The unforgettable scene in which the young publisher dances and clowns in front of the distinguished staff he has just bought away from a rival paper is curiously like a report I have recently read of Welles fooling around, telling wild stories, being the life of the party on the set of *The Trial.* Kane lived his whole life in front of an audience; so does Welles.

Every discussion of *Citizen Kane,* or of any other Welles movie, is sure to bring up his camera sense. In *Kane* there is the brilliant pseudo newsreel of the great man's death, the Senate investigation scene that is modeled on the inquisition of J. P. Morgan, the wide-angle lens that is supposed to approximate the eye's normal scope (and which for the first time required ceilings to close off the sets), the bold cutting that snaps the picture from one perspective to the next, the persistent low-angle shots that make Kane seem to tower above lesser men—and the audience. All such matters are handled with a sureness that is astonishing in a man making his first picture. We are back again to the gift of instant accomplishment—like knowing how to invest a bare stage with the highest dramatic tension, how to use the mechanics of radio with such deftness as to turn a stock thriller into an hour of public terror. It

Hard-bitten: Harry Lime in *The Third Man,* 1950

Jealous: Othello on the London stage, 1951

Troubled: in the film trilogy *Three Cases of Murder,* 1955

Vicious: international financier with a dubious past in *Mr. Arkadin,* 1955

Betrayed: the exiled monarch in *King Lear,* 1956

Hortatory: Father Mapple the preacher, *Moby Dick,* 1956

constitutes an instant feel for the nature of the vehicle; the effect is dazzling virtuosity.

But there is a price to be paid. Welles has said that anyone can learn the whole of movie technique in four hours. That is not true—though it may be approximately true for Welles. But if Welles learned the technique in something like four days, he has never quite assimilated it, in the sense that he is no longer self-conscious about the tool at his command. A child prodigy is applauded for his improbable skill with adult equipment; no one asks whether he is achieving adult results. But an adult should not go on indefinitely parading dexterity. It is characteristic of Welles that one is repeatedly aware of the effects he is creating. Whether it is the deliberately unreal sleigh party in *The Magnificent Ambersons,* or the studied irony of the Lucullan picnic and the eerie horror of the house of mirrors in *Lady from Shanghai* (there was a fake snowfall, a grotesque picnic, and an infinity of mirrors in *Kane,* too; Welles's tricks repeat themselves), or the architectural kaleidoscope of *Othello,* or the extreme contrivance of the angle shots used in *Touch of Evil,* or the nine hundred desks stretching to infinity in *The Trial*—however effective such devices may be technically, they divert the audience from what is being done to who is doing it. "Welles is at it again," we note indulgently, and thus he wins attention for himself at the expense of his creation.

I do not think that Welles means to do this; but then I do not think that he meant to be an adult prodigy. Events like the necessity to defy the United States Government over *The Cradle Will Rock,* like discovering in *Julius Caesar* a knife to use against Hitler, like being called a broadcasting menace to the sanity of the entire country, like incurring the senile rage

of the world's most phobic publisher, froze him in the role of prodigy. And it is the nature of a prodigy to be the master magician of whatever art he enters; only occasionally is he a master artist. Welles was that in *Kane,* though even that picture, for all its bravura screen effects, is not essentially a movie. It could be a novel, or a play; it lacks the cumulative power of an on-going visual flow that occurs when someone really exploits the genius of the camera—when, for example, John Huston makes *The Treasure of the Sierra Madre.*

Welles created his best stage productions back in the thirties, and he made his best picture in 1940. *The Magnificent Ambersons,* which followed *Kane,* seems curiously implausible and uncertain today, but Welles claimed that the point was edited out of it in his absence, and he broke with RKO over its release in truncated form. His other Hollywood pictures are superior Hollywood products; indeed, they often look like Hollywood outdoing itself. *Macbeth* and *Othello,* both filmed abroad, contain gimmicks designed to make Shakespeare work on the screen. The gimmicks in *Macbeth* are the removal of the scene to the barbaric era of the original legend and the portrayal of Lady Macbeth as a priestess of blood and lust. The results are striking, but the poetry does not transport as readily as the setting and the Elizabethan preoccupations come oddly from half-savage lips. The gimmicks in *Othello,* in addition to the aforementioned architectural dazzle, were to choreograph the action like a ballet and to suppose that Iago is motivated by impotence. The effect is a sadly diminished tragedy. There was a lot of Welles in these films; it is a question whether there was enough Shakespeare.

1: CULVER; 2: KEYSTONE PRESS; 3–4: CULVER; 5: MARTHA HOLMES; 6–11: CULVER; 12: ROGER CORBEAU

geful: corrupt sheriff
'ouch of Evil, 1958

Bewildered: a television
commentator in *The
Roots of Heaven,* 1958

Tyrannical: a Mississippi
papa in *The Long
Hot Summer,* 1958

Persistent: an imperson-
ation of Clarence Darrow
in *Compulsion,* 1959

Merciless: the Advocate
in *The Trial,* 1962–63

Forensic: a lawyer, one
of two roles by Welles in
Crack in the Mirror, 1960

Over the years Welles has been acting a great deal, here and abroad. He can play any part that is slightly bigger than life. He was the famous Harry Lime in *The Third Man;* an aging Southern gentleman in that curious transmogrification of Faulkner, *The Long Hot Summer;* a fictional version of Clarence Darrow in *Compulsion;* Benjamin Franklin in *A Royal Affair at Versailles.* He directed and took the title role in *Mr. Arkadin* (from his only novel), and it is the one Welles I have seen that I would call a clear failure—pretentious, obscure, and unamusing (which last is a fault almost unknown in Welles). There have been other parts. By chance I came upon a recent paragraph from Italy reporting the suppression of a film and the imprisonment of its director on the ominously inquisitorial ground of defamation of the state religion. This was *La Ricotta,* a movie within a movie about the crucifixion, in which Welles plays a film director.

He has said that his next picture will be about an aging film director, once great, now in eclipse; a romantic who cannot adapt to the narrow and canny realism of the "cool" generation. Kane was not Welles, nor will this old man be—but Welles has been a director most of his life and a romantic since birth.

Which, finally, brings the subject back to *The Trial.* The opportunities it afforded Welles to behave like a prodigy are obvious and legion. Kafka's nightmare world is a magic box for camera trickery and visual surprises, for baroque décor and bizarre characterizations. There have been complaints that Welles woefully overvisualizes a book which was visually almost barren. But I have always thought that I "saw" a good deal in the novel, and by and large the scenes evoked by Welles seem to me no violence to Kafka's intent.

The picture goes astray because Welles is a romantic—and, I think, an optimist. He cast Anthony Perkins, a yearning juvenile, in the lead, as though he thought K were a romantic hero. And he got from Perkins a remarkably solid performance. Nevertheless, Kafka's story of a man who is the law's victim because he is the utterly lawful man becomes the tale of a student rebel, the sort of young man who looks as though he couldn't care less about the law and its institutions. In the book the law devours its most ardent disciple; in the picture the totalitarian police pick up a potential dissident (and quite properly, given the viewpoint). That is an idea for a picture, but it is not Kafka's idea. Nor did Kafka have it in mind to warn his public against the imminence of atomic war—he was dealing with a horror of the soul. The mushroom cloud at the end of the film is another example of the boy scout in Welles; he has never been able to pass a soapbox without jumping up for a brief exhortation.

Nevertheless, the failure of *The Trial* comes much more from a gulf between the temperaments of author and director than it does from a prodigy's self-bemusement with the dexterity of his technique. If he does make that movie about the romantic director in a cool world, he will have a subject that corresponds to his own instincts. It could mark the end of the adult prodigy and the debut of the full-grown artist. The magic creations of his youth may seem very far in the past, but after all, Orson Welles is only forty-eight.

Robert Hatch, a regular contributor to HORIZON, *is the film critic and literary editor of* The Nation.

By OLIVER MILLAR, *Deputy Surveyor of the Queen's Pictures*

The Queen'ſ

HORIZON presents a panoramic view of the world's greateſ

One of its earlier Surveyors described the English royal collection of pictures as "a lone and proud surviver." The works of art collected by so many royal and princely families all over the Continent have, one by one, been dispersed or turned into public possessions. The Queen's pictures, on the other hand, have preserved their integrity and still reveal to us the changing enthusiasms of a succession of royal collectors from the close of the Yorkist age to the present day. If the collection has suffered many misfortunes—not the least of them the grievous dispersal of many of its finest treasures after the execution of Charles I—it is still of absorbing interest to the historian, as well as to the student of English taste, providing a vivid record of royal diversions, foibles, likes and dislikes, over the past four hundred and fifty years.

Inevitably so personal an assemblage will contain gaps. There are almost no good French eighteenth-century pictures; Constable and Turner are unrepresented; there are no impressionist or post-impressionist pictures. To compensate for this, however, the Crown still possesses superb examples of Italian Renaissance painting; one of the most magnificent displays in existence of Dutch seventeenth-century painting; indisputably the most important collection of works by Canaletto; and the finest collection in the world of English portraits, headed by unrivaled private "holdings" in Holbein and Van Dyck. Broadly speaking, the collection falls into two main categories: as Sir Walter Scott said, after seeing George IV's pictures at Windsor in 1826, there are "some fine paintings, and some droll ones." The backbone of the royal collection is formed by the chain of royal portraits of English sovereigns from Henry V to the present day and a host of their friends and relations, fellow-sovereigns, allies, and prospective brides. Onto this main stem practically every sovereign and many royal princes have grafted pictures of a more universal importance, but behind the walls on which hang George IV's Rembrandts, his father's Canalettos, and Charles I's Van Dycks you will still find those droll princes who fascinated Scott: "ill-coloured, orang-outan-looking figures, with black eyes and hook-noses, in old-fashioned uniforms."

The earliest inventories of the royal pictures were drawn up late in the reign of Henry VIII and in the reign of his son, Edward VI. They reveal that the Crown already owned many mythological scenes and religious canvases, although almost the only subject picture identifiable from the lists is the little anti-papal allegory attributed to Girolamo da Treviso, in which the Evangelists stone the prostrate figure of the Pope. The nucleus of the collection was the set of little portraits of the late Plantagenets and the early Tudors. The portraits of Henry V, Henry VI, Edward IV, and Richard III seem to perpetuate some *ad vivum* impression of the sitters' appearance.

No artists are named in the inventories of the Tudor collection; in fact, although Holbein has been associated for so long with Henry VIII, there is no evidence that the King owned any single portrait by him apart from the famous *Duchess of Milan*, now in the National Gallery in London. Holbein's principal work for the Crown was the legendary wall-painting in the Privy Chamber at Whitehall, ex-

Pictures

Queen Elizabeth II, by Pietro Annigoni

rivate collection, reflecting the taste of English monarchs through the centuries

ecuted in 1537 as a demonstration of the achievement and power of the new dynasty. It was destroyed in the fire at Whitehall in 1698, but from the famous "Chatsworth" cartoon for part of it and from the little copy of the whole, commissioned from Remiqius van Leemput by Charles II in 1667, it is possible to catch something of the awe-inspiring effect this demonstration of royal *terribilità* must have had on visitors to the palace. Apart from the well-known pageant pictures at Hampton Court, the most important portraits to survive from the early Tudor collection are of Edward VI and Elizabeth I at Windsor, probably by the same artist. They combine in a most delicate manner an understanding of the sitter's nature with a demonstration of the royal bearing—and something of the strains implied therein—in these young monarchs.

Sixteenth- and seventeenth-century visitors to England were impressed by the pictures in the royal palaces. "Masterly paintings" in many of the rooms at Hampton Court in 1592; "manie fayre galleries, stately furnished wth most artificiall and dilectable pictures, tables, and such like princely ornaments" at Whitehall in the same year; "many beautiful pictures" at Hampton Court in the early days of James I: these are some of the comments.

There is little evidence that Elizabeth I had added works of great artistic merit; and there seem to have been few, if any, direct links between the Crown and the leading European painters of this period. The Duke of Urbino had sent Henry VII the little Raphael of *Saint George and the Dragon,* which is now in Washington, and in 1553 the Queen

of Hungary had lent Mary I a portrait by Titian of her husband, Philip II. The impression one gains of the collection in the time of James I is of a mass of historical pictures, genealogies, maps, and a dignified royal portrait gallery.

With the accession of Charles I in 1625 we come to a turning point in the history of English connoisseurship.* Even the wife of a political adversary described him as "a most excellent judge and a great lover of paintings, carvings, gravings, and many other ingenuities." Charles had grown up under the influence of a group of men at his father's court who were effecting a revolution in matters of taste. Later, as king, Charles I and his immediate circle kept in touch with all the leading artistic movements across the Channel. He himself sat to Velázquez; Rubens, Van Dyck, and Jordaens were in his service; he owned superb modern Italian paintings; his bust in marble was carved by Bernini; and two of the first Rembrandts to leave Holland were set up at Whitehall.

In the development of the King's tastes the Duke of Buckingham and the Earl of Arundel wielded strong influence. Arundel's tastes were primarily for the Renaissance painters of Germany and the Netherlands. These preferences the King respected and partly shared. He owned magnificent portraits by Holbein, Arundel's favorite painter (including the famous *Erasmus,* now in the Louvre); he was presented by the City of Nuremberg with Dürer's *Self-portrait* (now in the Prado) and *Portrait of His Father,* and by the Dutch States-General with Mabuse's *Adam and Eve* (Hampton Court). Buckingham's less austere tastes embraced Caravaggio and his followers; his enthusiasm for Rubens and, above all, Titian

* See "The Prince of Patrons," HORIZON, July, 1961.

deeply influenced the young prince. In 1621 a consignment of pictures for the Duke had included Titian's great *Ecce Homo* (Vienna), and in the following year the Venetian ambassador in London, writing for his government a "character" of Charles, said "he loves old paintings, especially those of our province and city."

Prince Charles made the most of his "Spanish marriage" visit in 1623, attending sales and meetings of connoisseurs, sitting to Velázquez, and buying such pictures as Titian's *Girl in a Fur Wrap* (Vienna). On his departure Philip IV of Spain gave him Titian's *Venus of the Pardo* (Louvre), with which he had been particularly smitten.

Just before his accession a list of the Prince's pictures was drawn up, a microcosm of his future collections: the Trinity Altarpiece by Van der Goes; Holbein's *Erasmus*; Titian's *Charles V*; and a new *Self-portrait* by Rubens, still at Windsor, and painted, as the artist himself wrote, for "the Prince of Wales, of all the Princes of the world, the greatest lover of painting." And while he was in Spain the Prince had given orders "for certain patterns to be brought out of Italy and sent to us into England for the making thereby a Suit of Tapestry, which drawings as we remember are to cost near upon the point of £700"—drawings which were no less than the celebrated Raphael Cartoons.

Once upon the throne the King set seriously about enriching his inherited collection. Naturally he received presents from friends at home, from his relatives overseas, or from those, like Cardinal Barberini, who were courting his interest. Agents went abroad especially to acquire works of art for the King; and his residents, special envoys, and diplomats had instructions to keep their eyes open on the King's behalf, to negotiate directly with artists, and to keep their friends at home informed about the state of the arts in other countries. Arundel picked up the two Dürers at Nuremberg on the way back from an embassy to the Holy Roman Emperor; and in the early 1630's Sir Robert Kerr returned to London with two Rembrandts for the King.

Of the King's direct purchases by far the most notable was the acquisition, in two installments and in great secrecy, of the famous collection of the Gonzaga dukes of Mantua. At a cost of just over £18,000 Charles secured a great range of Renaissance masterpieces—Raphael, Titian, Andrea del Sarto, and Correggio were superbly represented—and of modern Italian masterpieces by Carracci, Caravaggio, and Feti, among others. An outstanding item in this huge purchase was the *Triumph of Caesar*, by common consent Mantegna's greatest work; this noble evocation of the Roman world survives at Hampton Court and, with Raphael's Cartoons, comprises the most splendid monument to the King's tastes. Perhaps the most vivid impression of the quality of the works of art that were coming into the possession of Charles I and his fellow connoisseurs can be gained by reading of the exchanges between them. The third Earl of Pembroke, for example, gave the King a Parmigianino and re-

HENRY VIII (*1509–1547*): *Late in Henry's reign the first inventories of the royal collection were begun, but did not include the artists' names. A dignified portrait (1) of Edward IV (1461–1483) was probably painted from life, and the intricate pageant picture The Field of the Cloth of Gold (2), in the 16th century. The small anti-papal allegory The Evangelists Stoning the Pope (3), one of a number of religious subjects, is attributed to Girolamo da Treviso, but the painter of Elizabeth I (4) remains unknown.*

CHARLES I (*1625–1649*): *Britain's most discerning and energetic royal patron, Charles bought much art and encouraged many Continental artists. A detail from the Trinity Altarpiece (5), by Hugo van der Goes, portrays James III of Scotland and his son; another detail is from one of the famous Raphael Cartoons (6), now in the Victoria and Albert Museum. Van Dyck anticipated the rococo with his Cupid and Psyche (7). One of Charles's finest acquisitions was a series on the Triumph of Caesar (8) by Mantegna.*

GEORGE III (*1760–1820*): *Earnest, stubborn, highly moral, this monarch expanded the royal collection. One of his favorite painters was the American Benjamin West, from whom he commissioned The Departure of Regulus (9); another was Gainsborough, who completed a series of fifteen outstanding portraits of the royal family, ten of which appear here (10) in the manner arranged by the artist. The King assigned Zoffany to some "royal conversation pieces" like Queen Charlotte and two of her children (11).*

GEORGE IV (*1820–1830*): *"The first gentleman of Europe" showed striking personal taste; he particularly liked portraits, such as that of Admiral Rodney by Sir Joshua Reynolds (12), Gainsborough's painting of three princesses, George's sisters (13), and Sir Thomas Lawrence's heroic Archduke Charles of Austria (14). George's passionate purchases of Dutch and Flemish art included two noble canvases: Ter Borch's conversation piece The Letter (15) and Shipbuilder and His Wife (16) by Rembrandt.*

VICTORIA (*1837–1901*): *Between them the Queen and her consort, Prince Albert, added a vast store of pictures to the collection. Shown here are Gozzoli's brilliant primitive The Death of Simon Magus (17), acquired by Prince Albert; Frith's Ramsgate Sands, of which this (18) is a detail; Landseer's sentimental painting of three dogs and a macaw, Dash, Hector, Nero, and Lorey (19); and a portrait of Victoria and her cousin, Victoria de Nemours (20), by F. X. Winterhalter, a court painter whom the Queen greatly admired.*

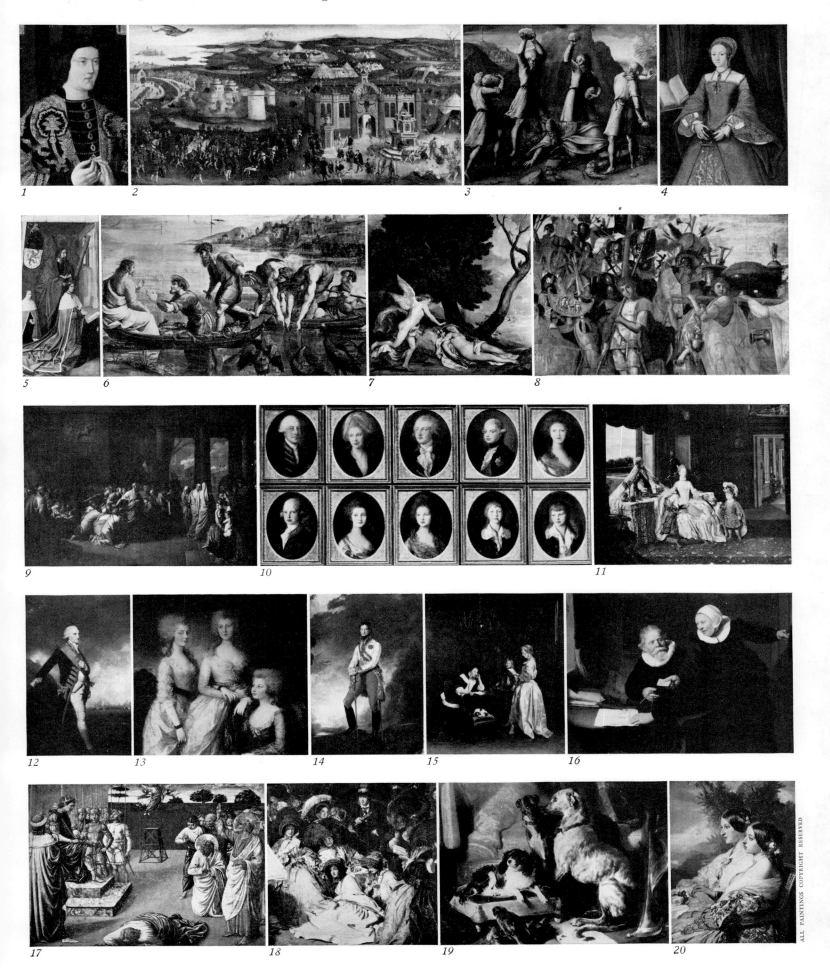

95

ceived in return Giorgione's *Judith*; the fourth Earl gave the King Raphael's *Saint George* in exchange for the volume of Holbein's portrait drawings which Pembroke generously made over to Arundel; Charles I got the Wilton Diptych in exchange for a portrait of himself; and the King was prepared to give up to the Duc de Liancourt Holbein's *Erasmus* and a Titian that had belonged to Donne in order to secure Leonardo's *Saint John*.

In the disposition of works of art within the King's houses most of his less important pictures remained at Windsor, Oatlands, and Nonesuch; fine Tudor and Jacobean pieces, with some of his best modern pictures, at Greenwich; and the cream of the collection at Hampton Court, Somerset House, St. James's, and Whitehall. In the small cabinets works of art of all kinds on a small scale were arranged in prodigal confusion. In the quiet of the King's more private apartments at Whitehall, however, the lucid arrangement of Renaissance masterpieces reveals the King's personal likes. His Titians included *The Entombment, Christ at Emmaus,* and *Allegory of Alfonso d'Avalos,* all now in the Louvre; *The Pope Presenting Jacopo Pesaro to Saint Peter* (Antwerp); and *Girl in a Fur Wrap, Saint Margaret,* and *Venus with the Organ-player,* now in the Prado.

The King's devotion to Venetian painting was closely linked with his choice of contemporary painters. His long admiration for Rubens culminated in the commission to paint for the ceiling of the new Banqueting House at Whitehall a vast allegory of the Stuart conception of Divine Right, in a style based on the great Venetians of the previous century. And Van Dyck, who created the ineradicable image of the King and his court, had been deeply influenced by his early study of Titian, the painter for whom, above all others, Charles had such a passion. An English contemporary outside the King's circle described Van Dyck as *"autem Titiani imprimis aemulus"* ("closely rivaling Titian"). Much of the significance of the great series of portraits painted for the King by Van Dyck, portraits of the King himself, of his wife, children, and friends, lies in their reinterpretation of Titian, in a subtlety unknown hitherto in the English portrait, and in a technical brilliance and a delicacy of color that foreshadow such painters as Watteau and Gainsborough in the eighteenth century. This is seen particularly clearly in the lovely *Cupid and Psyche,* where the distillation of Titian and Rubens produces a remarkable premonition of the rococo, especially of Boucher.

Within a few weeks of the King's execution the new republican Council of State proceeded with a detailed valuation of all the royal goods. The new government realized that so great a collection could be kept intact only with difficulty, and they organized its dispersal in an effort, which we should not unthinkingly condemn, to raise money for the fleet and to pay off the army of creditors left by the royal family. As a result, many of Charles I's finest pictures left the country, never to return.

A large number of paintings nevertheless remained in England during the interregnum, and these were reassembled so that the palaces of Whitehall and Hampton Court should not look unworthy when the monarchy was restored in 1660. Charles II and his brother James II inherited something of their father's tastes, and among the fine pictures that came into their possession was Holbein's wonderful *Noli Me Tangere.* As a patron, James II, who had been Duke of York, seems to have been more active than his brother. The famous "Beauties" by Lely were painted for his first Duchess; his love of the sea led him to commission from the two Van de Veldes a fine series of paintings of naval actions, and his Catholic zeal to employ Kneller to paint his masterpiece, the celebrated *Chinese Christian,* for the King's Drawing Room at Windsor. William III, Queen Anne, and the first two Georges left their mark on the royal collection, but not until George II's elder son, Frederick, a Prince of Wales who never reigned, do we come to a royal patron worthy to be compared with Charles I.

Since he died at the age of forty-four, the Prince of Wales necessarily acquired fewer works than did his son George III; he did not epitomize the taste of an age as his grandson George IV was to do later; but he had a spontaneous flair for pictures and, in common with George IV, he took a deep, personal delight in the arts. Whereas his father was content to entrust his features to such painters as the aging Kneller, Jervas, or Shackleton, the Prince went immediately to the painter with the liveliest style in London, Philippe Mercier. Prince Frederick enjoyed visiting the studios of painters, and he seems to have been easy, unpretentious, and kind in his dealings with artists and craftsmen. His encouragement of the fashionable French portrait painter J. B. Vanloo brought about a rococo enlivenment of the mortifying conventions of the English state portrait. In commissioning from English painters such as Charles Philips and John Wootton pictures of himself and his friends at convivial gatherings or in the hunting field, he was fostering the growth of two favorite English genres, the conversation piece and the sporting piece. Wootton's finely painted hunting scenes, in particular, bridge the gap between his master, the Dutchman Jan Wyck, and the early works of Stubbs. The Prince's feeling for Italian pictures would have found favor with Horace Walpole. He purchased fine examples of Teniers, Jan Bruegel, Gaspard Poussin, Claude, Murillo, and Ribera, and also shared his mother's interest in early English pictures. She had bought, about 1734 or 1735, the superb Holbein of Sir Henry Guildford (reproduced on the cover of this issue), the finest portrait now surviving in England from Holbein's first years there.

But the pictures he liked best were undoubtedly those of the previous century; his finest acquisitions were the pair of superb landscapes by Rubens, *Winter* and *Summer,* and a magnificent series of Van Dycks. These included the noble

TEXT CONTINUED ON PAGE 105

On the following pages: A portfolio in gravure of masterworks from the Queen's Pictures

(ABOVE) DUCCIO DI BUONINSEGNA (1255–1319): "CRUCIFIXION"

(OVERLEAF) PETER PAUL RUBENS (1577–1640): "THE FARM AT LAEKEN"

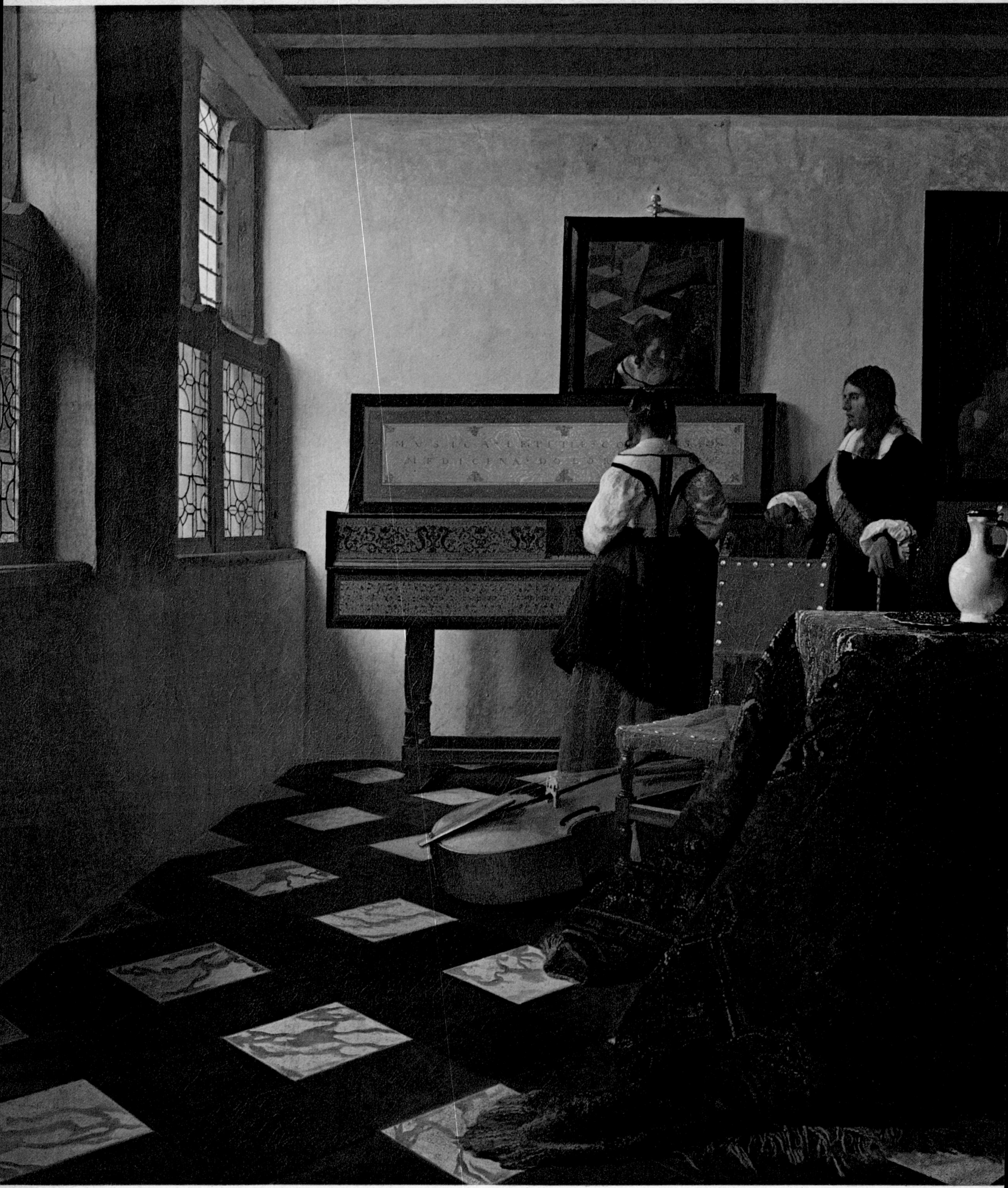

(ABOVE) REMBRANDT VAN RIJN (1606–1669): "THE LADY WITH A FAN"

(LEFT) JAN VERMEER (1632–1675): "THE MUSIC LESSON"

(OVERLEAF) GEORGE STUBBS (1724–1806): "PRINCE OF WALES' PHAETON"

CANALETTO (1697–1768): "THE PIAZZETTA, VENICE"

and early *Saint Martin,* two sumptuous female portraits from Van Dyck's most accomplished late phase, and the brilliant double portrait of Thomas Killigrew with a companion, who may be Lord Crofts. The Prince's achievement as patron and collector is surely the finest thing in his short life.

Prince Frederick's son, George III, was brought up under the influence of Princess Augusta, Frederick's wife, and of the Earl of Bute, and was surrounded by his father's pictures, furnishings, and silver. Inevitably George III inherited at least a predilection toward good pictures, an interest in the portraiture of his own family, and a feeling that it was his duty to leave a mark on the royal collection. He left an impress on it, indeed—one that is strongly felt today. It is unlikely that he shared his father's or his son's delight in painting for its own sake; his activities as patron and collector were probably governed by other considerations, but it is only fair to recall Lord Melbourne's remark to Queen Victoria in 1838 that "George III, though accused of the contrary, was excessively fond of the Arts." With his young wife, Charlotte of Mecklenburg-Strelitz, he made a clean break with the past history of the collection when they took over Buckingham House. On May 24, 1762, Walpole wrote to George Montagu, "the King and his wife are settled for good and all at Buckingham House and are stripping the other palaces to furnish it."

Buckingham House and Kew Palace were, therefore, to be filled with the finest pictures in the inherited collection and with the pictures the King set himself to acquire. "Large commissions were sent to Italy," wrote John Watkins, the Queen's biographer, "for the purchase of paintings, antiques, and other curious articles to enrich this favourite mansion." His greatest single purchase came in 1762, when he secured almost the whole collection formed by Joseph Smith, the British consul in Venice, of which the jewel was Vermeer's *The Music Lesson,* now the principal Dutch masterpiece in the Queen's collection (see plate III in the portfolio). Nor had Smith neglected his opportunities in Venice. Among other and lesser Venetian works, he had accumulated the world's largest and finest collection of Canalettos: many of his small, rather conventional views on the Grand Canal; a series of famous Venetian churches and public buildings; some charming *capricci*; the Thames seen from Somerset House; a set of dazzling Roman views; and, most important, six large canvases from Canaletto's early years, before his vigorous brushwork and brilliant sense of light and atmosphere became formal and stereotyped (see his *Piazzetta, Venice,* opposite).

George III and his Queen never got on with Sir Joshua Reynolds and in the first part of their reign entrusted their portraits, and those of their children, to Allan Ramsay's sensitive talent. The King was a devoted father and husband, and his strong family feeling led him to commission from Zoffany a series of delightful royal conversation pieces in which he and the Queen are seen with their children in different royal interiors or in a royal park. But the most beautiful royal likenesses of this period are those by Gainsborough, for whom the royal family seems to have had great affection. In 1781 the artist exhibited at the Royal Academy his full-length studies of the King and Queen, which are perhaps the most subtly brilliant English royal portraits since the days of Van Dyck; and in 1782 he painted at Windsor the delightful set of oval portraits of the by now enormous family that are still hung at Windsor in accordance with Gainsborough's instructions to the Academy's hanging committee of 1783.

In complete contrast the works painted for the King by Benjamin West displayed a high-minded and severely moralizing approach to painting. West's choice of heroic subjects of courage, self-sacrifice, and constancy, his belief that the value of painting lay "in assisting the reason to arrive at earnest moral influences," strongly appealed to the King. When he first met the young painter, "sedate in his affections, and deeply impressed with the sanctity of principle," he admired a picture West had painted of Agrippina with the ashes of Germanicus and commissioned from him a picture of the *Departure of Regulus;* he called for a copy of Livy and read West the story that he was to illustrate. Thereafter West covered acres of canvas for the King on classical, religious, medieval, and modern subjects. The regrettable aspect of West's work is that he could not actually paint, but his subject matter and its relation to George III's character and to the taste of the time give it considerable interest today.

George III's son—first as Prince of Wales, later as Prince Regent, and finally as George IV—was aware of the educational value of his collection, made it available to students, and often lent his pictures to exhibitions at the British Institution. His patronage of living artists and his pursuit of old pictures were the result of a spontaneous enthusiasm and an eye for quality that place him in the distinguished company of Charles I and Prince Frederick; it is odd that two of England's least satisfactory sovereigns have been the most effective and enthusiastic patrons and collectors. George IV had no feeling for Italian pictures or for primitives, but he did build up a collection of Dutch and Flemish pictures of the seventeenth century which has never been surpassed, in which the majority of pictures are splendid examples of their kind, and which survives intact as one of the principal glories of the Queen's collection. In addition the water-color interiors of Carlton House at that time show how carefully the King placed his pictures in relation to the decoration of some of those charming rooms. George IV's was, in other words, an intensely personal collection and still stands indefinably apart from the rest of the Queen's pictures.

Like his father, the Regent collected portraits of his family; perhaps his loveliest acquisition was the exquisite triple painting by Gainsborough of his three eldest sisters, shown at the Royal Academy in 1784. He also surrounded himself with portraits of his raffish early associates. He had inherited his grandfather's love of sporting life, and built up a superb collection of such scenes, including a set of celebrated pieces by Stubbs (see plate V in portfolio) and others. The family passion for military matters was his also, and he was regarded as the greatest authority in Europe on military uniforms and equipment; with this went a profound interest, and a rather pathetic and vicarious pride, in the heroic events over which, as Regent, he chanced to preside.

He reveled in the part of host at the 1814 celebrations of the Bourbon restoration and the arrival in London of the Czar, the King of Prussia, and Field Marshal Blücher; he had been painted as a young man in Beechey's huge *Review*, dressed in the uniform of Colonel of the 10th Light Dragoons; and he ventured to commission Stroehling to paint him as a Field Marshal on horseback. This picture he gave to Lady Conyngham, and it is still at Slane Castle; but, alas, Stroehling's picture of him as the Black Prince has been lost. His enthusiasm for the heroic actions of the period led him to commission large canvases of the battles of Vitoria and Waterloo, and he owned Turner's *Trafalgar*, which he later gave to Greenwich Hospital. He hung the East Anteroom at Carlton House with portraits of such celebrated men of action as Nelson and Rodney.

The East Anteroom thus contained the embryo of the Regent's greatest single achievement as a patron and a most splendid monument to the overthrow of Napoleon: the set of portraits, later placed in the Waterloo Chamber at Windsor, of the sovereigns, commanders, and statesman who had contributed to the Emperor's final defeat. The most important portraits were entrusted to Sir Thomas Lawrence, who rose magnificently to the occasion with varied, remarkably unmonotonous, and splendidly painted canvases in a dashing neo-baroque style, an arresting blend of heroics and romance. Unlike his father, the Prince admired Reynolds; he was a special patron of Hoppner; and he even bought *The Mock Election* from the eccentric Haydon, but he seems totally to have ignored Constable and—except for *Trafalgar*—Turner as well. The British artist whom, apart from Lawrence, the Regent patronized most generously was David Wilkie.

Although the Prince was spending fairly heavily in the first years of the nineteenth century, his collection of old pictures was not at that date of very high quality; but by the time he became Regent in 1811, he was fast becoming one of the principal collectors of the day, benefiting, as did other collectors, from the breaking up of many collections on the Continent during the Napoleonic Wars. The acquisition in May, 1814, of pictures from the collection of Sir Francis Baring so raised the standard at Carlton House that the Prince in the same month threw out many of his former possessions and sent them to Christie's auction rooms.

The Prince Regent owned very good examples of the Italianizing Dutch landscape painters so popular at this period—Berchem, Both, and Du Jardin—and two superb Van der Heydens, together with fine conversation pieces by Ter Borch, De Hooch, and Adriaen van Ostade. The two Van de Veldes and Metsu, Wouvermans, and Hobbema are well-represented. The Prince's Cuyps are exceptional, and it would be impossible to select the finest of his Rembrandts: the choice would probably rest between the *Shipbuilder and His Wife* of 1633, the *Lady with a Fan* of 1641 (see plate IV in portfolio), and the *Noli Me Tangere* of 1638, which was acquired in an exchange and is practically the only religious picture in the Prince's collection. Among his Flemish pictures are pieces by Teniers, in which the quality of color and handling is consistently good. He bought, in 1821, the *Farm at Laeken* (see Plate II), the quality and condition of which are again unsurpassed, and, in 1824, Rubens's *Landscape with Saint George*, that charming idyll set near the Thames. In a peculiarly happy moment he bought Van Dyck's famous triple portrait of Charles I, which had been sent to Rome for the assistance of the sculptor Bernini and had remained there until 1802. One of his last purchases, in 1829, the year before he died, was Claude's *Rape of Europa*.

William IV, who came to the throne in 1830 for a brief seven years, did not have his elder brother's feeling for works of art. On seeing one of George IV's pictures he remarked, "Ay, it seems pretty—I daresay it is—my brother was very

The Art-filled Palaces

The Queen's Pictures are principally housed in the four great royal palaces shown here. The new gallery itself is at Buckingham Palace, first occupied by George III. Windsor Castle, a royal residence for nine centuries, contains old portraits, the Canalettos, and many Holbeins and Van Dycks. St. James's Palace, London, is the official residence of the monarch and the seat of such offices as that of the Surveyor of the Queen's Pictures; Hampton Court, beloved of Henry VIII, has Tudor pageant pictures, Mantegnas, and Holbein's Noli Me Tangere.

Buckingham Palace

Windsor Castle

fond of this sort of nicknackery. Damned expensive taste, though."

On the occasion of George IV's birthday in 1827, his sister-in-law the Duchess of Kent had written to him: "The only offering I could think of making on this day is the resemblance of our little angel." The little angel was, of course, Princess Victoria, who came to the throne ten years later and, with the Prince Consort, added another memorable chapter to the history of the royal collection. There is no doubt that the two very different personalities of the Queen and Prince were perfectly combined in their attitude to the arts.

From the pages of the Queen's journal in the years before her marriage we read of her own water colors and etchings, of the fun she got out of looking at fine houses, such as Chatsworth or Haddon, and of her regular visits to exhibitions. When she talked with Lord Melbourne, she expressed a taste for Italian pictures and a desire to buy some. She was, therefore, the perfect counterpart to the serious-minded Prince, of all royal patrons the most dedicated to the service of the arts and the most consistently and professionally devoted to their welfare in England and to promoting the part they should play in the life of the nation. The Queen and the Prince spent many hours arranging their possessions and especially enjoyed looking at the prints and drawings in the Library or rearranging the miniatures. The Prince initiated, with the Queen's Surveyor, Richard Redgrave, a detailed inventory of the collection; it is still in daily use in the Surveyor's office. He also made careful dispositions of all the pictures, which the Queen, after his death, would never allow to be altered or undone.

The vast number of works added by the Queen and the Prince fall into two main categories: the contemporary Victorian paintings, and the Italian, German, and Flemish primitives which were the Prince Consort's great personal contribution. The work of the Pre-Raphaelites seems never to have appealed to the Queen. The painters who most pleased her and her husband were F. X. Winterhalter, who produced a steady succession of thoroughly competent portraits of the royal family, varying from large groups to small sketches; and Sir Edwin Landseer, a painter of much greater natural ability, who produced enchanting pictures of the royal children, of royal dogs and other pets, and a famous series recording the royal couple's life in the Highlands.

Perhaps the greatest service done by the Prince Consort to connoisseurship in England was his determination to make primitive paintings known to a wider public than the handful of collectors who then admired them. After exhibiting the collection of his cousin, Prince Oettingen-Wallerstein, at Kensington Palace in 1848, he bought the pictures himself and arranged that after his death the finest should go to the National Gallery. The Cranachs, the great Montefeltro group by Justus of Ghent, the Gozzoli of the death of Simon Magus, the Fra Angelicos, the superb Duccio (see first plate in portfolio)—to mention a few—constitute an enduring monument to the most serious of all English royal collectors.

Although the Prince Consort was the last of the heroic figures in the history of the royal collection, it is now perhaps more vitally alive than at any time since his death. His arrangements were modified, entirely for the good, by Edward VII; since then many important pictures have been acquired, particularly since the Second World War, and a large number have been cleaned, some with spectacular success. Research on the history of the Queen's pictures has continued more intensively than ever before. Growing numbers of people have seen more and more of the royal pictures over the last fifteen years, and the opening last year of the Queen's Gallery at Buckingham Palace has provided the public with a continuously changing spectrum of the treasures of the royal collection.

The inventories and other documentary sources, as well as the more important printed works, on which this article is based, are described in the Bibliography of Mr. Millar's The Tudor, Stuart and Early Georgian Pictures in the Collection of Her Majesty The Queen, *published this year as the first volume in the new Catalogue Raisonné of the Queen's pictures.*

Hampton Court

KEYSTONE

St. James's Palace

Sumer's Language of Love

INANNA

GU-DA-LA *(embrace)*

GIS-GU-ZA *(throne)*

MU-TI-IN *(bridegroom)*

HI-LI-ZU *(your allure)*

LAL-AM *(honey)*

KU-KU-DA *(sweet)*

SHA-ZU *(your heart)*

KI-AG *(love)*

SHU-TAG *(caress)*

SIR-SHA-HUL-LA
(songs that rejoice the heart)

AMAUSHUMGALANNA

NA *(bed)*

KULIANNA

AMA-MU *(my mother)*

SIPAD *(shepherd)*

DUMUZI

O Ye Daughters of

New light on the Biblical book commonly known as Solomon's Song of Songs has been cast by current archaeological discoveries in Sumer, the Mesopotamian kingdom that flourished in the third and second millenniums B.C. On the clay tablets excavated there love poems have been found remarkably similar in form to that most sensuous of Biblical texts. The Song of Songs is like no other book in the Old Testament. In fact, it seems to be nothing more than a loosely organized collection of love poems. No wonder there has been considerable debate about the propriety of including it in the Biblical canon at all; although once included, it came to be regarded as an allegory, with Jahweh in the role of the lover and the Hebrew people in the role of His bride.

Modern scholarship, however, cannot accept this fanciful interpretation. To judge from what we now know of the history and culture of the ancient Near East, there is good reason to believe that at least some portions of the Song of Songs were originally sung during the *hieros gamos,* or "sacred marriage," between a king and a votary of Astarte, the Canaanite goddess of love and procreation.

The Canaanite rite itself had roots deep in the history of Mesopotamia; it derived from the Tammuz-Ishtar cult, which was in turn a counterpart of the Dumuzi-Inanna cult of ancient Sumer. In the course of recent years a considerable amount of Sumerian literary material has been unearthed which emphasizes the importance of the Sumerian legacy to Biblical literature. For some time past a highly competent German expedition has been making significant discoveries at Erech, an important Sumerian city-state two hundred miles south of modern Baghdad; while an expedition of the University Museum of the University of Pennsylvania has found tablets of basic importance for the understanding of the Dumuzi-Inanna cult at Nippur, which was the cultural center of Sumer, located about sixty miles northwest of Erech.

Dumuzi was a prominent ruler of Erech in the third millennium B.C. The tutelary deity of the city-state was Inanna, a goddess who throughout Sumerian history was deemed to be primarily responsible for sexual love and fertility. As the Sumerians became more nationally minded, however, there arose the seemingly quite plausible and not unattractive idea that the king of Sumer, no matter who he was or from what city, must become the husband of the life-giving goddess Inanna of Erech. Eventually the dogma was actually put into ritual practice with the consummation of a marriage ceremony, probably repeated every New Year, between the king and a specially selected priestess from Inanna's temple.

To lend prestige and authority to the rite, it was desirable to attribute the symbolic marriage to an earlier time, and the honor of being the first mortal to wed the deity not unnaturally fell to Dumuzi, the Erech ruler who had become such a memorable figure in Sumerian legend. Moreover, the premarital courting and wooing of Inanna by Dumuzi became a favorite subject of Sumerian bards. We now possess numerous examples of their poems on this theme (two of them are reproduced on these pages) showing the extent to which the Biblical canticles were anticipated. To be sure, aesthetically speaking, the songs in Solomon's Song of Songs, with their concrete, rich, and impassioned imagery, are far superior to their stilted, repetitive, and relatively unemotional forerunners. But there is little doubt today that more than a few of the expressions, implications, situations, and allusions in the Biblical masterpiece have their origins in ancient Sumer.

Samuel Noah Kramer is Clark Research Professor of Assyriology at the University of Pennsylvania and the author of History Begins at Sumer.

found erotic lyrics, precursors of the sensuous Song of Solomon

Sumer!

One of the most charming of the Sumerian love songs is recorded on a two-column tablet (a portion of which appears at left) now in the Hilprecht collection of the Friedrich-Schiller University of Jena in East Germany. It might almost be entitled "Fooling Mother." In the poem, after an amorous tête-à-tête, Inanna, the Sumerian Venus, pleads with Dumuzi, her mortal sweetheart and future husband, who is also variously known as Kuliana, Amaushumgalanna, and Kulienlil:

> Come now, set me free, I must go home,
> Kulienlil, set me free, I must go home,
> What can I say to deceive my mother,
> What can I say to deceive my mother Ningal?

Dumuzi has a ready answer:

> I will tell you, I will tell you,
> Inanna, most deceitful of women, I will tell you.
> [Say] 'My girl friend took me with her to the public square,
> There a player entertained us with dances,
> His chant, the sweet, he sang for us.'
> Thus deceitfully stand up to your mother,
> While we by the moonlight take our fill of love;
> I will prepare for you a bed pure, sweet, and noble,
> The sweet day will bring you joyful fulfillment.

Another of the best preserved Sumerian love lyrics is inscribed on a tablet from Nippur now in the Istanbul Museum of the Ancient Orient. It would probably have been recited by a priestess of the goddess Inanna, as a part of the rites of holy marriage between the goddess and King Shu-Sin, who reigned in Sumer about 2000 B.C.

> Bridegroom, let me caress you,
> My precious caress is more savory than honey,
> In the bedchamber, honey filled,
> Let us enjoy your sweet allure,
> Lion, let me caress you,
> My precious caress is more savory than honey.
>
> Bridegroom, you have taken your pleasure of me,
> Tell my mother, she will give you delicacies,
> My father, he will give you gifts.
>
> Your spirit, I know where to cheer your spirit,
> Bridegroom, sleep in our house until dawn,
> Your heart, I know where to gladden your heart,
> Lion, sleep in our house until dawn.
>
> You, because you love me,
> Give me pray of your caresses,
> My lord god, my lord protector,
> My Shu-Sin who gladdens Enlil's heart,
> Give me pray of your caresses.
>
> Your place goodly as honey, pray lay [your] hand on it,
> Bring [your] hand over it like a gishban-garment,
> Cup [your] hand over it like a gishban-sikin garment.

By SAMUEL NOAH KRAMER

The
HIDDEN,
The
UNKNOWABLE,
The
UNTHINKABLE:

Of Sir Richard Burton, his explorations, his eccentric tastes,

Richard Francis Burton, born in the nineteenth century, rightfully belonged to the Renaissance, and should have been contemporary with Sir Walter Raleigh and Sir Francis Drake. Instead he was trapped in the century least capable of appraising his talents, confined and penalized by the pruderies of Victorian England, praised for only the most obvious of his abilities, and condemned for a curiosity as prodigious as it was penetrating. He was an explorer of immense courage and endurance who penetrated the sacred cities of Mecca and Medina at great risk and wrote a detailed description of his experiences. He was the first European to discover and properly identify Lake Tanganyika.

Like many other distinguished authors, he visited America and wrote a book about his adventures. He lacked the animus of Frances Trollope and Charles Dickens, and looked at everything with a friendly and generally unprejudiced eye. He was not captivated by the political processes, as were Alexis de Tocqueville and Lord Bryce, but concentrated instead on exotic phenomena such as the American Indian and the American polygamist. The flourishing Mormon Zion in Utah drew him like a magnet, and the resulting *City of the Saints* was the best book on the Mormons published during the nineteenth century.

As a disciplined journalist, Burton saw and recorded everything wherever he went, buttressing his notes with the wide background reading of a dedicated scholar. He was also an ethnologist, archaeologist, linguist, poet, and translator. Besides this he was an amateur botanist, zoologist, doctor, and surgeon, and incidentally a superb swordsman and celebrated raconteur. He published thirty-nine volumes on his travels and explorations, three grammars of Oriental languages, five volumes of folklore. He translated several volumes of poetry, and achieved enduring fame with his great sixteen-volume edition of *The Arabian Nights,* which he larded with ethnological notes to make it a treasure house on the culture of the East.

"Discovery is mostly my mania," he once wrote. And although his journeyings, particularly his hazardous search for the source of the White Nile, would seem to indicate a passion for geographical discovery, actually his real preoccupation was with the people.

His mania was for discovery of the hidden in man, for the unknowable, and inevitably the unthinkable. Here he ran afoul of British society, which was already having difficulty digesting the findings of Charles Darwin, and which greeted with glacial hostility the tentative gropings of the precursors of Sigmund Freud.

For human communication in his travels Richard Burton would go to extraordinary lengths. First he eliminated the language barrier. As a boy he had alternately lived in France and England; he was not quite English in England and not quite French in France. France he always preferred. "England," he said, "is the only country where I never feel at home." But once having tasted the pleasure of mastering a language, he found it a necessity. With each new tongue he would first master the elementary grammar, then absorb a minimum vocabulary of eight hundred words, memorizing from notes he kept in his pockets, always practicing aloud. Reading followed, and sedulous listening to master the tricks of pronunciation. After two months of this regimen, he tells us, "the back of the language was broken."

But being a linguist was not enough. For absolute penetration of a new culture Burton liked to go into disguise. In India he masqueraded as a Bushiri merchant, in Egypt as an Indian doctor, in Arabia as a Pathan, in Ethiopia as a Moslem. He was always in danger of being exposed, which no doubt greatly heightened the excitement; but he was artful enough to pose as someone not quite native, a traveling peddler, a pilgrim, always a stranger from some distance so that his language, dress, and mannerisms would go unchallenged. The rewards were extraordinary; so, as it turned out, were the penalties.

As a lieutenant in the British army in India, he had nothing but contempt for his fellow officers who remained aloof and indifferent to the exotic culture surrounding them. The first day of his arrival in Bombay he hired a tutor to improve his Hindustani, and he went on to become proficient in Marathi, Sindhi, Punjabi, Persian, and Arabic. Eventually he attacked Turkish, Armenian, Telugu, and Pashto. As a trusted intelligence officer under Sir Charles Napier, he mingled with the natives, and was able to supply his chief with valuable information about native temper and political intrigues.

By FAWN M. BRODIE

Captain Sir Richard Burton, K.C.M.G., a man of many roles, is shown above in his favorite Arab dress. (Confuse him not with any other Richard Burton.)

and his ever-watchful wife

"The European official in India seldom, if ever, sees anything in its real light," he wrote, "so dense is the veil which the fearfulness, the duplicity, the prejudice, and the superstitions of the natives hang before his eyes. . . . Hundreds serve through what they call their 'term of exile' without once being present at a circumcision feast, a wedding, or a funeral." In return many of his fellow officers repaid him with contempt of their own, calling him "the white nigger" because he was seen so often with Indian friends.

Napier at one point requested Burton to make a report on several homosexual brothels in Karachi, which he feared might be corrupting the British troops stationed in the city. Burton agreed, with the stipulation that the report be kept confidential and not forwarded to Bombay. The subsequent study, explicit and detailed to a degree extraordinary even for a gifted intelligence officer, did not upset the shockproof, Rabelaisian Napier. But his less worldly successor read it with consternation and forwarded it to Bombay with the recommendation that Burton be cashiered. Burton escaped dismissal at the time. Later, however, when he asked for a post for which his linguistic attainments eminently qualified him, the report was maliciously attached to his application and the job was given instead to an officer who had only a smattering of Hindustani. Burton at this point realized that his career in the British army was permanently ruined.

According to Norman M. Penzer, the able bibliographer of Burton's writings, the report was finally "in all probability burned." But the rumor that "something wrong" was known about him haunted Burton all his life, unshakable and vaguely degrading. There were to be many burned manuscripts in Burton's history, and every fire robbed his biographers of material vital to a just appraisal of the man.

Richard Burton was born at Barham House, Hertfordshire, March 19, 1821, the eldest of three children. His father, Lieutenant Colonel Joseph Netterville Burton, born in Ireland though of English descent, had retired early from the army "with little money and no reputation." His mother, Martha Baker, was a timid, unselfish woman who had inherited a modest property in her own name. Most of Richard's childhood was spent in Tours, France, save for

a brief unsatisfactory period in a preparatory school at Richmond, England. Later, as his father toured the Continent in desperate search of a cure for his chronic asthma, wandering became for the Burtons a way of life.

Richard, Catherine, and Edward were tutored in an erratic fashion, but their chief accomplishment seems to have been the languages they absorbed. Richard and his brother were lively, mischievous, and at times ungovernable; Burton described them once as ducklings in a nest of hens. "Like most boys of strong imagination and acute feeling," he wrote frankly, "I was a resolute and unblushing liar; I used to ridicule the idea of honor being in any way attached to telling the truth. . . . That feeling continued for many a year, and at last, as very often happens, as soon as I realized that a lie was contemptible, it ran into quite the other extreme, a disagreeable habit of scrupulously telling the truth whether it was timely or not."

In later life Burton's reputation for telling the truth, even when it was supremely tactless, nevertheless continued to be paralleled by his predilection for relating tall tales. He delighted in shocking, particularly audiences of Victorian women, who too often believed his stories of personal seduction, killing, and cannibalism, interspersed as they were with authentic details from his wilder escapades. Late in life he confessed freely that he had never killed anybody, and the closest he ever came to eating human flesh seems to have been his organizing the Cannibal Club in England, a frankly crackbrained offshoot of the Royal Geographical Society.

No one seems to have misunderstood Richard Burton more than his father, who wanted to turn him and his brother into clergymen. Edward was sent to Cambridge and Richard to Oxford with this end in view. Burton later described all his schooling in England as "a nightmare." "In consequence of being brought up abroad, we never thoroughly understood English society, nor did society understand us."

Expelled from Oxford for going to a steeplechase against college orders and refusing to be properly penitent, he returned to his family in France and begged for an army career. His father capitulated and purchased a commission for him in the 18th Bombay Native Infantry, and Burton went off jubilantly to Asia, his doting mother meanwhile complaining that "it was just as if the sun itself had disappeared."

In the Indian Army he won a reputation for being a great swordsman, drinker, brawler, and practical joker. He wrote witty, insulting verse lampooning his superior officers. He compiled a fake grammar to prove that the members of an obscure tribe in northern India with marked Semitic features were in reality the lost Ten Tribes of Israel, and very nearly published it as authentic. He kept for a time a colony of monkeys, treating them like humans and studying their sounds, hoping to penetrate the mystery of their communication. He compiled, he said, a vocabulary of sixty words, but this was burned, along with all his Asian costumes, books, and manuscripts, in a warehouse fire in London.

Burton made no secret of his heartbreak over the ruining of his Indian career. "I had been seven years in India," he wrote, "working like a horse, volunteering for every bit of service, and qualifying myself for all contingencies. . . . Sick, sorry, and almost in tears of rage, I bade adieu to my friends and comrades in Sind. My career in India had been in my eyes a failure, and by no fault of my own."

Returning to England, he took refuge in writing. Four books emerged from his pen in two years: *Scinde, or the Unhappy Valley* (1851); *Sindh and the Races that Inhabit the Valley of the Indus* (1851); *Goa and the Blue Mountains* (1851); and *Falconry in the Valley of the Indus* (1852). They did not sell well: his style lacked felicity, his humor was too sardonic, his irony too biting, and there were long stretches of description that were simply dull. Most of the fascinating lore he had absorbed when disguised as a merchant in the Indian bazaars he left out altogether. In his later writings, when he dared include explicit material on sexual customs by somewhat concealing it in an appendix, he still ran the danger of having it dropped at the last minute by a timid editor—as in his *First Footsteps in East Africa,* where his Appendix IV, on infibulation, was listed in the table of contents but omitted from the published text.

Burton had many friends in both the aristocratic and Bohemian circles in London, but he was considered by many to be eccentric, un-English, and indefinably dangerous. Even his personal appearance contributed to this reputation. He was a tall man, with immense shoulders, powerful muscular arms, and a massive head that seemed all the bigger for the extravagant size of his drooping mustaches. The fashionable novelist Marie Louise de la Ramée, better known by her pen name, Ouida, said he looked like Othello and the Three Musketeers blended into one. "His mere presence in a clubroom," she wrote, "made the ordinary clubmen seem small." Arthur Symons described him as having "a tremendous animalism, an air of repressed ferocity, a devilish fascination," with "the sullen eyes of a stinging serpent." Wilfrid Scawen Blunt called him "a black leopard, caged but unforgiving."

In 1853 Burton crossed the Channel to Boulogne, where he finished

African kings received Burton with ceremony but some hauteur, as above. "You are a good man, but too angry," one told him.

the writing of his *Complete System of Bayonet Exercises,* a small study which eventually revolutionized bayonet drill in all the armies of Europe. It was in Boulogne that he met the tall, blond Isabel Arundell, a member of the Catholic aristocracy of England, a girl of considerable beauty and a proud, independent, and authentically romantic spirit. She later described their first, accidental encounter: "He looked at me as though he read me through and through in a moment, and started a little. I was completely magnetized, and when we had got a little distance away, I turned to my sister, and whispered to her, 'That man will marry me!'"

They met formally, danced once together, and Isabel reverently put away to keep forever the gloves and sash she had worn that night. Though he made no further effort to pursue her, she vowed with a passion worthy of the most sentimental of British novels that she would marry no one else. "I *cannot* marry any of the insignificant beings around me," she wrote in her diary. "Where are all those men who inspired the *grandes passions* of bygone days? Is the race extinct? Is Richard the last of them? Even so, *is he for me?*"

Unaware of the excitement he had inspired, Burton shortly set forth on the voyage that was to bring him his first real fame. With the blessing of the Royal Geographical Society he set out for Arabia, hoping not only to penetrate the holy cities but also to explore a large desert area as yet unmapped by Europeans. In Alexandria he posed as an Indian doctor. Burton was a good amateur physician who knew all the harmless palliatives and had no compunction about prescribing them. In some ways he was in advance of the professionals, abhorring the use of leeches for bloodletting and urging filters and distillers to purify water against dysentery. In the role of doctor he was able to perfect his Arabic, to add to his familiarity with the minutiae of Moslem etiquette and ritual, and incidentally to satisfy his curiosity about harem life.

Although at least twelve Europeans had penetrated the holy cities of Mecca and Medina in disguise and lived to tell of the experiences, the risk of death if caught was real, and Burton took every precaution, including that of having himself circumcised. Posing as a Pathan born in India of Afghan parents, Burton began the journey determined to fulfill every ritual requirement. He was tormented by heat and desert winds, lamed by a nasty foot infection, and threatened by the general hazards of a journey that invariably cost the lives of many Moslem pilgrims. The resulting three-volume account of his adventures, *Personal Narrative of a Pilgrimage to Al-Medinah and Meccah,* was a truly remarkable historical document. His insights into Moslem thinking were original and perspicacious; his details, whether written in admiration, contempt, or fury, were exact.

The book made a sensation in England. But instead of returning to enjoy his fame, Burton was off to another holy and forbidden city, Harar, the capital of Somaliland. "When I spoke of visiting it," he wrote, "men stroked their beards, and in Oriental phrase declared that the human head once struck off does not regrow like the rose." Undismayed, he put on Moslem garb, penetrated the city, and talked freely with the king, persuading him of Britain's wish for friendly relations, and after ten days escaped without mishap. This only sharpened his appetite for more. He planned a second expedition with several British officers, among them Captain John Hanning Speke. Almost at the outset they were ambushed by Somali natives. One man was killed, Speke was badly wounded, and Burton had a javelin hurled through his jaw.

In the forbidden Arabian city of Medina (seen here in a print based on a Burton drawing) risk of death was real. Burton went as an Indian doctor.

be welcomed home by some little corner of the Great World, which takes a pride in your exploits. In the contrary condition you are a waif, a stray; you are a blaze of light without a focus. Nobody outside your own fireside cares."

Although they were soon engaged, Burton could not bring himself to the finality of marriage until he had finished his conquest of the upper Nile. This, he knew, would take almost three years. Isabel, as a devout Catholic, was troubled by her hero's ill-disguised atheism, and her mother was appalled at the idea of having Richard Burton for a son-in-law. Still, the thought of marriage to anyone else was insupportable, and Isabel promised to wait until his return.

Forced to return to Aden for medical aid, Burton hurriedly wrote up the account of both adventures. The resulting *First Footsteps in East Africa; or An Exploration of Harar* (1856) went almost unnoticed in England, for the Crimean War had broken out and overshadowed interest in everything else. Burton went off to the Crimea, where he served on General Beatson's staff in the Dardanelles. He was never able to get to the front.

Once the war was over, he determined with characteristic audacity to put an end finally to the centuries-old mystery of the source of the White Nile. All expeditions attempting to trace the great river from Egypt had ended in the cataracts and vast morasses of the South, with heat, malaria, and hostile natives taking a dreadful toll; and the origins of the annual September flood that inundated the lower valley were still, in 1858, "the greatest geographical secret after the discovery of America." No one had much improved on the map drawn by Ptolemy, which suggested that the Nile rose in two great lakes, said to have been visited by a Greek merchant named Diogenes in the first century A.D. Burton knew that rumors of these lakes had been somewhat substantiated by vague reports from missionaries, and determined to find them by striking westward from the Zanzibar coast. It was an area wholly unexplored and unmapped by Europeans, but somewhat familiar to slave-trading Arabs.

Back in England, enlisting help from the Foreign Office and the Royal Geographical Society for his expedition, Burton again accidentally met Isabel Arundell and discovered, doubtless to his astonishment, that she had been nursing her *grande passion* for years. Although he had been in love many times, Burton had continued to escape marriage. The courtship of a Persian girl he had loved deeply in India had been cut short by her tragic death. British mothers whose daughters he had admired had found him too poor or had been frightened by his reputation. By now both his parents were dead, and he was shattered by the illness of his brother, who had been badly beaten in a native riot in Ceylon and had become, as a result of the brain damage, hopelessly mute.

Now, at thirty-seven, famous and eligible, though not rich, he seems to have discovered that he was also very lonely. "It is a real advantage," he wrote later, "to belong to some parish. It is a great thing, when you have won a battle, or explored Central Africa, to

When he left her, she became, in true Victorian fashion, extremely ill, pouring out her lament in her diary: "It is infamous the way half the men in the world live and die, and are never missed, and, like a woman, leave nothing behind but a tombstone. By ambition I mean men who have the will and power to change the face of things. I wish I were a man: if I were, I would be Richard Burton. But as I am a woman, I would be Richard Burton's wife. I love him purely, passionately, and devotedly. . . . Whatever the world may condemn in him of lawless actions or strong opinions, whatever he is to the world, he is perfect to me; and I would not have him otherwise than he is—except in spiritual matters. This last point troubles me."

Burton went to Africa in late 1858 with the thirty-year-old John Speke, who had been wounded with him in Somaliland. This was to prove a disastrous choice. Speke was a passionate game hunter and eager explorer, and also a passable geographer, but he had no competence as a linguist. He was stubborn and competitive, and prone to nurture secret grievances. As Alan Moorehead has pointed out in *The White Nile,* "Burton needed a disciple and instead he got a rival." Moreover, Speke was apparently subject to depressions. "Before we set out," Burton noted later, "he openly declared that, being tired of life, he had come to be killed in Africa." Burton, on the other hand, was too easily contemptuous and free with criticism, too insistent on being right by virtue of being leader.

On the journey both men were plagued with terrible illnesses, succumbing to almost every disease of the jungle. They suffered also from tropical rain, heat, insects, fatigue, and malnutrition, as well as constant fear of attack from hostile natives. After fourteen months they found themselves on the shores of Lake Tanganyika. Unable to explore it completely because of opposition from the natives, by no means certain that it was the Nile source, Burton nevertheless was content to end the exploration. Exhausted and ill, he decided to convalesce in Kazeh, where there were Arab traders with whom he could talk, to put his notes in order, and to gather data on the native languages.

Speke pushed on alone to discover the second great inland lake—Victoria—and returned to tell Burton he was certain he had found the true source of the Nile. Jealous and arrogant, Burton scorned the younger man's claims, pointing out that Speke had neither explored the lake nor ascertained its outlet. Tension between the two men over the issue quickly became intolerable. There were no supplies, however, for further exploration to settle the question, and the men began the hazardous return journey. It was a nightmare of sickness and distrust.

When they got to Aden in March, 1859, Burton dallied, permitting

Burton met Isabel Arundell in 1853. She waited eight years to marry him, while he roamed from Mecca and Africa to Salt Lake City.

Speke to arrive in London before him. Ignoring his promise to make a joint report with Burton before the Royal Geographical Society, Speke went at once to the president, Sir Roderick Murchison, and convinced him he had discovered the Nile source singlehanded. In a speech before the Society he again described the expedition in these terms, incidentally attacking Burton and belittling his role. The group at once invited Speke to head a new expedition to Africa and raised £2,500 for it. All this was skillfully managed before Burton's arrival twelve days later.

Back in London, Burton found himself largely forgotten or ignored. "I shall never forget him as he was then," Isabel Burton later wrote. "He had had twenty-one attacks of fever, had been partially paralyzed and partially blinded; he was a mere skeleton, with brown yellow skin hanging in bags, his eyes protruding, and his lips drawn away from his teeth." Full of compassion, she helped nurse him back to health, meanwhile protesting indignantly among her influential friends against what she believed to be Speke's unpardonable betrayal.

Burton had often said "he required two, and only two qualities in a woman, namely beauty and affection." He had also written that he admired them "soft-bending and relaxed." In Isabel he found the first and second qualities but manifestly not the third. Despite all her protestations of adoration and devotion she could be a stubborn and exacting woman. Though she had vigorously repudiated all the suitors selected by her mother up to this point, she refused now to marry Burton without her mother's consent. The fact that her father liked Richard immensely and the uncomfortable realization that she was nearing thirty were not enough. Mrs. Arundell remained adamant, and the arguing and pleading went on for almost a year.

Meanwhile Burton worked feverishly at his manuscript of the African expedition, which he hoped would win back some of the honors Speke had so neatly taken unto himself. His two-volume *Lake Regions of Central Africa* (1860) showed that he had developed into a fastidious and thorough scholar. Here is the geography, biology, geology, and meteorology of the area through which they passed; also the foods, customs, and adornment of the natives, as well as their tribal fetishism, polygamy, internal slave traffic, and techniques of warfare. Nothing seems to have escaped him—nothing, that is, but the true source of the Nile. On this subject he chided Speke for his effrontery and insisted that only future exploration

would settle the matter. It was true that nothing had been proved absolutely, but Speke happened to be right and Burton wrong, and in the end this circumstance tarnished Burton's reputation as an explorer.

As the controversy heightened in London, Burton began winning friends for his side. But the Royal Geographical Society continued to side with Speke, and Burton found he had "opened up the oyster for the rest to take the pearl." Suddenly, without warning even his still temporizing fiancée, Burton left England. A note delivered after his departure told her he was off to explore another holy city, this time the mecca of the Mormons in the valley of the Great Salt Lake. He would be gone, he said, for nine months, during which time she was to make up her mind finally about their marriage. "If once you really let me go, mind, I shall never come back," he said, "because I shall know that you have not got the strength of character my wife must have."

The Mormons at this time were considered a great curiosity in England. Since the murder of Joseph Smith in Illinois in 1844, and the subsequent dramatic exodus to the desert isolation of the great inland sea, the sect had flourished beyond the wildest predictions. Brigham Young had become virtual sovereign over an immense empire. Mormon missionaries had had an astonishing success in Great Britain and Scandinavia, almost thirty thousand converts having emigrated to America between 1840 and 1860. The fact that the Mormons now openly admitted that they were practicing polygamy did not seem to deter many. Charles Dickens, visiting an emigrant ship chartered specifically for Mormons, took a hard look at the "single women of from thirty to forty . . . obviously going out in quest of husbands, as finer ladies go to India. That they had any distinct notions of a plurality of husbands or wives, I do not believe," he said.

The Mormon capital had become a must on the itinerary of transcontinental sightseers. The French botanist Jules Remy and the British naturalist Julius Brenchley had visited it in 1855. William Chandless had written a friendly account in the same year. Horace Greeley had filled many columns in his New York *Tribune* describing his Mormon interviews in 1859. Richard Burton came in 1860; Mark Twain would follow in 1861, Fritz Hugh Ludlow in 1864, and Ralph Waldo Emerson in 1871, all save Emerson turning out books or articles as a result of their exposure to the Mormon phenomenon. Of all these none wrote so sagacious and thorough a study as Richard Burton.

During his three weeks in Salt Lake City Burton seems to have sampled everything permitted; he talked incessantly to Mormons and gentiles; he attended Mormon services and dances; he looked at prices in the stores, wandered through the cemeteries, read a prodigious amount of Mormon and anti-Mormon literature, and interviewed Brigham Young.

Polygamy, of course, excited him most; it was the reason for his seeking out the Mormons in the first place. But he brought to his research the urbanity of a scholar already intimately acquainted with polygamous marriages of every conceivable variety in Africa and the Near East. He had seen African chiefs with as many as three hundred wives, and societies where polygamy was unlimited; he had visited one tribe where only the chief was allowed many wives and his subjects were punished for infractions of a puritanical sexual code by having their eyes gouged out. Among the Moslems, he had studied harem life as had no other European of his time. "The Moslem admits," he said, "that envy, hatred, and malice often flourish in polygamy, but asks in turn, 'Is monogamy open to no objections?'. . . As far as my limited observations go," he went on sagely, "polyandry is the only state of society in which jealousy and quarrels about the sex are the exception and not the rule of life. In quality of doctor I have seen a little and heard much of the harem. It very much resembles a European home composed of a man, his wife, and his mother."

One motive Burton listed for entering polygamy was economy; most Mormons would have been quick to disclaim it. "Servants are rare and costly; it is cheaper and more comfortable to marry them," he said crisply. "Life in the wilds of Western America is a course of severe toil: a single woman cannot perform the manifold duties of housekeeping, cooking, scrubbing, washing, darning, child-bearing, and nursing a family. A division of labor is necessary, and she finds it by acquiring a sisterhood."

Burton also hinted delicately at a more fundamental reason for the acceptance of polygamy by Mormon women, a puzzling phenomenon to many, which he was certain could not be explained merely by "promises of Paradise" or "threats of annihilation." He described on the one hand a certain type of British and American woman, "petted and spoiled . . . set upon an uncomfortable and unnatural eminence . . . aggravated by a highly nervous temperament, small cerebellum, constitutional frigidity, and extreme delicacy of fiber," and contrasted her with the Mormon wife, supreme in her domesticity and motherhood, surrounded by other women and masses of children, preferring the society of women to men in any case. To annotate this he quoted in full the astonishing defense of polygamy by Mrs. Belinda Marden Pratt, in which she emphasized that "nature has constituted the female differently from the male; and for a different purpose"; namely, motherhood, and that she needs "relief at regular periods, in order that her system may be kept pure and healthy." Mrs. Pratt shared her husband with six other wives; there were altogether twenty-five children. "All these mothers and children are endeared to me by kindred ties," she said, "by mutual affection, by acquaintance and association; and the mothers, in particular, by patience, long-suffering, and sisterly kindness." Burton admitted that Belinda Pratt showed

The last nineteen years of his life Burton and Isabel lived in Trieste. "I have domesticated and trained Richard a little," she wrote dotingly.

"little heart or natural affection," but applauded "the soundness of her physiology."

Many, notably Isabel, construed Burton's comments on polygamy as a defense of an infamous system. *The City of the Saints* was the first book Burton published after their marriage, and he turned the final editing over to her hand. She, for all her wit and charm, never understood her husband's irony, and consistently misread his detachment as approbation. It was a favorite saying with him, according to his biographer Thomas Wright, that "man is by nature polygamic, whereas woman, as a rule, is monogamic, and polyandrous only when tired of her lover. The man loves the woman, but the love of the woman is for the love of the man."

In a later book, *Explorations of the Highlands of the Brazil,* he described a village with 20 per cent more males than females and noted jovially: "Is it not a waste of productive power? . . . Is it not lamentable to see men blinded by the prejudices of education, thus neglecting the goods the gods provide? Surely it is time for some Senhor Dr. Brigham Joven to arise in the land." The humor was lost on Isabel, who was editing the volume, and she made a spirited public protest in a special preface. "It is therefore time for me respectfully to assert," she said, "that, although I proudly accept of the trust confided in me, and pledge myself not to avail myself of my discretionary powers to alter one word of the original text, I protest vehemently against his religious and moral sentiments, which belie a good and chivalrous life. I point the finger of indignation particularly at what upholds that unnatural and repulsive law, Polygamy, which the Author is careful not to practice himself, but from a high moral pedestal he preaches to the ignorant as a means of population in young countries."

What Isabel Burton missed altogether in *The City of the Saints* was her husband's shrewd perception of what was missing in the Mormon plural marriage. "The choice egotism of the heart called Love," he said, "subsides into a calm and unimpassioned domestic attachment: romance and reverence are transferred, with the true Mormon concentration, from Love and Liberty to Religion and the Church. The consent of the first wife to a rival is seldom refused, and a *ménage à trois,* in the Mormon sense of the phrase, is fatal to the development of that tender tie which must be confined to two. In its stead there is household comfort, affection, circumspect friendship, and domestic discipline." The result, he said, was a pervasive atmosphere in Salt Lake City which could best be described as "gloom."

Similarly Isabel Burton misunderstood her husband's appraisal of Moslem polygamy. Moslems, he said, "do their best to countermine the ascetic ideas inherent in Christianity, are not ashamed of the sensual appetite, but rather the reverse." In his "Terminal Essay" to *The Arabian Nights* he developed the theme at length. "Moslems and Easterns in general study and intelligently study the art and mystery of satisfying the physical woman. . . . The mock virtue, the most immodest modesty of England and of the United States in the nineteenth century, pronounce the subject foul and fulsome: 'Society' sickens at all details; and hence it is said abroad that the English have the finest women in Europe and least know how to use them."

Burton was at his best in describing Brigham Young. He was astonished at Young's youthful appearance; though fifty-nine, he appeared to be about forty-five. With his marvelous eye for detail Burton came away from the interview with a total recall of face, hands, hair, clothes, mannerisms, and an astute judgment on Young's character. "The first impression left upon my mind by this short *séance*," he wrote, "was that the Prophet is no common man, and that he has none of the weakness and vanity which characterize the common uncommon man." He was impressed by the absence of bigotry, dogmatism, and fanaticism, by his cold, "somewhat bloodless" manner, by his sense of power. "There is a total absence of pretension in his manner, and he has been so long used to power that he cares nothing for its display. The arts by which he rules the heterogeneous mass of conflicting elements are indomitable will, profound secrecy, and uncommon astuteness."

Brigham Young in his turn seems to have found Burton impressive, and later escorted him about the city. When Burton asked if he could be admitted to the Mormon fold, Young replied with a twinkle: "I think you've done that sort of thing once before, Captain." They ascended the hill north of the city, where Brigham Young pointed out the chief buildings below, including the houses of his leading men and his own gabled Lion House, in which he kept many of his wives. At this point Burton complained facetiously that he had come all the way to Salt Lake City without a wife only to find that all the ladies had been captured by Mormon men. He waved his right hand toward the lake, saying mournfully: "Water, water, everywhere"—and then his left toward the city—"and not a drop to drink." Brigham Young laughed heartily, and they parted, apparently with great mutual respect.

Upon his return to London, Richard told Isabel bluntly she must choose between him and her mother or he would be off to India. Isabel, who had had nine months to reflect upon the chances of losing her hero altogether—and who had used the time to equip herself for becoming the wife of an adventurer by learning how to cook, to handle a fencing foil, to groom a horse, and to milk a cow—capitulated instantly. Three weeks later, January 22, 1861, they were married in a quiet, almost secret ceremony in the Bavarian Catholic Church. "We will have no show," Burton insisted, "for a grand marriage ceremony is a barbarous and indelicate exhibition."

Marriage brought to Richard Burton a wife who adored, admired, and defended him all her life, but who also worked strenuously to tame him. He repaid her with lasting devotion and respect, but he also escaped from her for long periods. Their marriage has been described repeatedly as one of the great enduring Victorian romances; Ouida, who knew them well, called it "a love-marriage in the most absolute sense of the word." Early in the marriage Richard ran the risk of wrecking it altogether by hypnotizing Isabel—daily, if we are to believe her biography—in an effort to find out what she was thinking. "He used laughingly to tell everybody," she wrote, "it's the only way to get a woman to tell you the truth." Later he boasted that he could hypnotize her from a distance of many miles and maintain a kind of telepathic communication.

Several months after their marriage, when it became clear that the active social life they were leading among the great houses of England would soon exhaust their meager resources, Burton accepted an obscure position as consul at Fernando Po, an island off the coast of West Africa chiefly important as a naval station for ships engaged in suppression of the slave trade. This was the best that the timid officials of the Foreign Office, who put respectability at the top of their requirements, dared offer the most courageous and distinguished explorer in England. The fever-ridden island was said to be certain death for English women, and Isabel stayed behind disconsolate in England, as she described it, "neither maid, nor wife, nor widow."

No British consul in any African post ever utilized his time and opportunities as well as Richard Burton during his four years at Fernando Po. He made repeated journeys into the interior of West Africa and wrote three absorbing volumes describing his experiences: *Wanderings in West Africa from Liverpool to Fernando Po* (1863), *Abeokuta and the Cameroon Mountains* (1863), and *A Mission to Gelele, King of Dahomé* (1864). The last, an account of the kingdom of the Amazons, is one of the best of the pioneer studies on African customs. Burton was fascinated with the spectacle of 2,500 women warriors who, he said, though "too light to stand a charge of the poorest troops in Europe," and who maneuvered "with the precision of a flock of sheep," nevertheless fought with great ferocity. Their battles consisted largely of raids on neighboring tribes for slaves, a practice Burton had been commissioned to discourage. He had small success in this. "You are a good man," King Gelele told him patronizingly, "but too angry."

In 1865 Burton was transferred to Santos in Brazil, where Isabel for the first time was able to make a home. They spent four years in Brazil, two in Damascus—which ended in trouble because of the intrigues of Syrian officials who came to dislike Burton—and finally nineteen years at Trieste. The Foreign Office considered him too independent, irascible, and tactless to be trusted with an important post. Nevertheless, it permitted him an extraordinary amount of freedom for travel and writing. Eventually, on his twenty-fifth wedding anniversary, he was knighted.

Meanwhile books continued to pour forth from his pen. His wife did much of the drudgery, copying, editing, and proofreading. At one point she wrote a lively, gossipy book of her own, *The Inner Life of Syria* (1875), which sold better than any travel book of her husband's. Burton wrote too hastily, often without order or discrimination. His books are too anecdotal and not sufficiently analytical to place him among the front ranks of the theorists in anthropology.

It was in his final years that Burton produced his greatest work. As early as 1852 he had planned a translation of the Arabian Nights' tales in collaboration with Dr. John Steinhauser. After Steinhauser's death in 1866 he continued collecting the tales, finding them "an unfailing source of solace and satisfaction . . . a charm, a talisman against ennui and despondency." He did little translation, however, until after 1879, when he was stimulated to action by the announcement of a forthcoming edition by John Payne. Burton was determined to translate the tales in their entirety, without any of the expurgation of all the previously published texts. "If anything is in any redaction of the original, in it should go," he wrote to Payne, urging him in the same direction. "Never mind how shocking it may be to modern and Western minds. If I sin, I sin in good company—in the company of the authors of the Authorized Version of the Bible, who did not hesitate to enter *literatim* certain passages which persons aiming simply at artistic effect would have eliminated."

The Burton edition *(A Plain and Literal Translation of the Arabian Nights' Entertainments, Now Entitled the Book of the Thousand Nights and a Night),*

Burton the eccentric, strikes a pose, about 1855. He had, said a contemporary, "an air of repressed ferocity."

though heralded by many journals as a monument of knowledge and audacity, was also attacked as indecent and filthy. The *Edinburgh Review,* in July, 1886, called it "an appalling collection of degrading customs and statistics of vice," a work "which no decent gentleman will long permit to stand upon his shelves. . . . Galland is for the nursery, Lane for the library, Payne for the study, and Burton for the sewers."

Undismayed, Burton went on to publish six supplemental volumes, replying to his critics with still more compendious notes on the erotic customs of the East. "The England of our day would fain bring up both sexes and keep all ages in profound ignorance of sexual and intersexual relations," he wrote, "and the consequences of that imbecility are particularly cruel and afflicting. . . . Respectability unmakes what Nature made."

The Nights was a surprising financial success, which gave Burton a special sardonic satisfaction. "I struggled for forty-seven years," he said, "I distinguished myself honorably in every way I possibly could. I never had a compliment nor a 'Thank you,' nor a single farthing. I translated a doubtful book in my old age, and I immediately made sixteen thousand guineas. Now that I know the tastes of England, we need never be without money."

Upon finishing *The Nights* Burton began to work on a new edition of *The Perfumed Garden of the Cheikh Nefzaoui,* an Arabic manual on the art of love. He had only a few pages left to finish when he died of a heart attack, on October 20, 1890.

At the moment of his death Isabel Burton called in a priest for the essential ceremonies, insisting that her husband had been at heart a true Catholic. She provided for elaborate Catholic funerals in Trieste and in England, and had his body placed in the Mortlake Catholic cemetery in an extraordinary tomb built in the shape of an Arab tent, decorated inside with tinkling camel bells and stars to imitate the desert night. She had, perhaps, forgotten what Burton wrote after walking around the Mormon cemetery in Salt Lake City: "The tombs, like the funeral ceremonies, are simple, lacking the 'monumental mockery' which renders the country churchyard in England a fitter study for farce than for elegy."

Burton had willed to his wife all his manuscripts and journals ex-

cept *The Perfumed Garden,* which seems to have been promised to F. F. Arbuthnot, Burton's partner in a society which was founded specifically for the publication of the erotic literature of the East. But when Isabel Burton sat down for the first time to read its contents, she was appalled. Later she confided to friends that her husband came to her three times in a dream and commanded her to burn it. And burn it she did. His manuscript of Catullus she then expurgated and retyped, and burned the original. She also purchased and destroyed as many copies as she could find of his *Stone Talk,* a long satirical poem castigating British politicians and containing a few strictures against Catholicism and marriage which he had published under a pseudonym in 1865. Finally she looked at the forty-year accumulation of diaries and journals, said by those who had been permitted to examine them to be better than his books, better even than his conversation, and which contained all the thoughts, caustic comments, reports of conversations, summaries of letters, and all the fascinating jottings of this great Rabelaisian adventurer. These, too, she added to the holocaust.

Then she wrote a biography of her husband in which she tried desperately to fashion him in the image of her own fantasy. She would have one believe that he was at heart a good Catholic, though his books are peppered with his mockery of superstition and priestcraft, whether Christian, Moslem, or heathen. "I ignore the existence of a soul and spirit," he had said publicly in 1878, "feeling no want of a self within a self, an I within an I." And in the "Terminal Essay" he had written: "The more I study religions the more I am convinced that man never worshiped anything but himself."

Isabel did her best to eliminate evidences of his curiosity for erotic practices, fearful lest he be thought vicious because he collected data on what Victorian England called vice. He was, she insisted, "in private life the most pure, the most refined, the most modest man that ever lived." It is a sad and ironic circumstance that Burton, for all his hunger for communication, for all his hypnotism and supposedly telepathic interchanges with his wife, never properly measured her capacity for destruction and never successfully established the communication that might have allayed it.

The best of Burton, then, is either burned or buried. But that which is buried, whether by being locked in the library cases specializing in privately printed editions or simply by being scattered among the thousands of pages of his travel books, is eminently worth unearthing. Our own century, it is to be hoped, will finally look at Richard Burton with the same kind of urbanity and detachment that he brought to the Arabs and the Mormons.

Fawn M. Brodie grew up in Utah in a Mormon community. This essay is the introduction to her edition of Richard Burton's The City of the Saints, *to be reissued shortly by Alfred A. Knopf, Inc.*

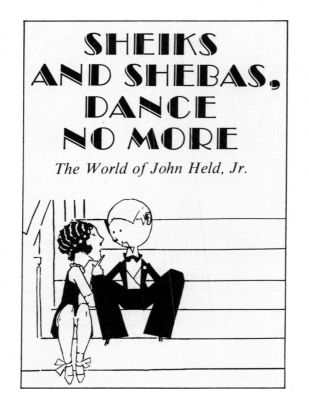

SHEIKS AND SHEBAS, DANCE NO MORE

The World of John Held, Jr.

It is always the autumn of 1926, the last Saturday in September or the first in October, the ivy leaves on the stadium wall crisping to scarlet, the sun still warm, the lucent air all blue and gold. It is a midwestern university, *the* midwestern university—mock-Gothic library and chapel, mock-classic classrooms, the lush tapestry-brick veneer of fraternity row. With the big game only hours away, the saxophones of the college band are giving anticipatory blasts between the chapel and the gymnasium.

Over that pied and milling campus the sunshine is almost tangible. The sheiks wear Fair Isle sweaters of gaudy intricacy, checked plus fours with tasseled socks, or gray flannels so bell-bottomed that they completely cover the saddle-strap shoes. Most of the sheiks are hatless, and their hair, parted in the middle, is lacquered with Slikum or Staycomb to a mirrorlike stiffness. The shebas have close-cropped, shingled hair. Beneath their sweaters or sheath dresses there is only the vaguest convexity of breast. Their knobby knees are topped by frilled garters, and fringed skirts sway above the knees.

A Theta Delt (one can tell by the Θ Δ X on his cap) is strumming "Bye Bye Blackbird" on his ukulele for a covey of shebas sitting on the library steps. They sit with legs apart, displaying the V-shaped pattern of their lace panties with provocative unconcern. A freshman, still marked with the grotesque innocence of Central High School (he will shed it before spring), passes timidly by the insouciant sophs and juniors, wearing a beanie branded with the numerals 1930. The date is, of course, part of his absurdity. For every sheik and sheba knows that 1930 will never come, that there will never be anything but here and now —this timeless moment throbbing to the beat of "The Varsity Drag." It is warm, mindless, immediate. It is the Plastic Age of Percy Marks's forgotten novel, of the quintessence of a thousand campus paper cut ups (*Bowdoin Bearskin, Dartmouth Jack O'Lantern, Notre Dame Juggler,* and the rest), of *College Humor*

with its: "College bred—a four-year loaf!" It is the world of John Held, Jr.

That nature imitates art is one of those paradoxes Oscar Wilde confected to startle the dinner tables in the 1890's. Since then it has been repeated so often that it has become a truism. Yet a truism, for all its acquired banality, may be none the less true, and art does in fact have a way of nudging nature. In any age there is first the amorphous urge toward a pattern, a malaise seeking an outlet. And always the artist appears to embody the age or the spirit of the time, whether it is Mr. Pope in his grotto at Twickenham or Mr. Eliot listening to the melancholy notes of St. Mary Woolnoth.

A generation before Held, Charles Dana Gibson sat at his drawing board, and at the command of his pen Gibson girls appeared like daisies on the American scene—haughty yet chastely alluring, an aureole of hair beneath their flowered pancake hats, and with floor-length skirts and leg-o'-mutton sleeves. There was a Gibson man as well, an earlier eternal undergraduate, who wore his varsity sweater inside out so that only the Y stitching showed, smoked a pipe, and was accompanied by a bulldog on a leash. He returned the Gibson girl's glance ardently, from afar—and he came to actuality in the person of Richard Harding Davis.

Gibson outlived his creation, even as Held was to outlive his. In the era when the sheiks and the shebas Charlestoned and black-bottomed their way through the pages of the old *Life,* Gibson continued to produce his fine-drawn society sketches for the same magazine. But his genteel figures, though the women shortened their skirts and bobbed their hair, appeared as pathetic revenants in the dazzle of the Heldian campus world.

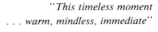

"This timeless moment . . . warm, mindless, immediate"

Curiously enough Held was about fifteen years older than the types he created. Nor did he himself ever attend college. He was born in Salt Lake City in 1889. At fourteen he started working as copy boy for a newspaper, and at fifteen sent his first acceptable cartoon to *Life.* Six years later, determined to be a cartoonist, he left for New York, arriving there with four dollars in his pocket. He managed to get a job in the art department of a newspaper and continued to draw cartoons in his spare time. "I was looking for success. I found it," he wrote later when he was making several thousand dollars a week as the tone-giving cartoonist for *Life, Judge,* and *College Humor.* But he had to wait fifteen years, until he was in his middle thirties, before he found what he had been looking for.

ILLUSTRATIONS BY JOHN HELD, FROM *Held's Angels,* © 1952 BY FRANK B. GILBRETH AND JOHN HELD; THOMAS Y. CROWELL CO., N.Y.

During the First World War Held served uneventfully in the Navy, and after he was discharged in 1919 went to work for the old *Life*. The prewar humorous weekly had grown stuffy, but now Robert Sherwood as editor and Robert Benchley as dramatic critic were to revivify it. At first, more than anything else, the pages reflected the uneasiness of the postwar period. They looked back nostalgically to 1914, welcomed the newly elected Harding as a symbol of "normalcy," resented the strikes and the High Cost of Living, feared the agitator, the Bolshevist, and the anarchist. Even the humor was uncertain of itself, much of it being a play on anachronisms, applying the situations of the mechanized modern world to the Stone Age or the Middle Ages. The captions beneath the cartoons tended to the old "he-she" variety, such as two young people in evening dress at a concert:

SHE: Tell me, are you fond of Brahms?
HE: Oh, very! But I think I like shredded-wheat biscuits even better.

"The new generation was Held's . . . hey-hey sayers to life"

During the transition period between the Armistice and the Coolidge prosperity John Held, Jr., remained one of the obscurer signatures in *Life*. Pseudo-primitive woodcuts were at first his favored medium, as if he sensed that the moment was not yet his. The small fillers fell to him, such as the sketches at the top of Benchley's drama page. It was in these tentative drawings that he began to feel his way into his distinctive style.

His moment came with the season of Coolidge prosperity, a season so warmly sunlit that few noticed the slanting rays were autumnal. The conflicts of the postwar adjustment period were over, 1914 with its fashions and its foibles had sunk below the horizon, the now was here. Intellectuals sitting in self-conscious exile at the Dôme drinking their cognacs might consider themselves the lost generation, but the new generation in America was Held's—sheiks in coonskins with hip flasks, shebas in helmet hats carrying tapered cigarette holders. They are models rather than caricatures, hey-hey sayers to a life that reaches its thundering climax in the cheering sections at the Saturday big game.

After the game there are the ritual dances along fraternity row. Over the fieldstone mantel of the fraternity-house living room stand the cabalistic Greek letters. In the corner the saxophones wail and a bulb flashes on and off in the interior of the bass drum to light up a windmill or a waterfall or a sailboat by moonlight painted on the drumhead. A few couples are dancing, a few

more are in the kitchen mixing drinks, but most are twined in each others' arms in the convenient alcoves or along the wide staircase as they neck with concentrated unconcern.

After the dance there is the ride home. Some of the dough-heavy sheiks may drive a Jordan Playboy, with port and starboard lights, but most settle for the modified Model-T, the tin-Lizzy touring with the top and windshield removed and its sides daubed with legends: *Four Wheels–No Brakes*; *Stop Me If You've Heard This*; *Enter by Rear*. Under the trees the last sheik parks with the last sheba for the last drink and the last neck. Yet for all this hip-flasked groping in the moonlight, it is somehow innocent, or almost so, and has the poignancy of everything that is brief.

The lengthening of women's skirts was the curtain ringing down on John Held's campus world, and it was the skirts rather than the stock market that marked the end. Sheiks and shebas danced no more. Held himself turned back to his earlier woodcut style and forward to the *New Yorker,* where with mock-primitive sophistication he illustrated the Frankie and Johnnie songs of the nineties. The Depression did not cut him down materially. With his first surge of success he had bought a stock farm in Connecticut, and he continued to live there through the thirties as the artist of *Pious Friends and Drunken Companions* and as a dapper country gentleman. Tall, dark, and still exuberant (heavily tattooed with eagles, girls, anchors, and roses), he often amused himself by tap dancing in public. Although in his illustrations he stuck to the archaisms of his woodcuts, in several volumes of short stories that he now wrote—*Grim Youth, The Flesh Is Weak*—he attempted, unsuccessfully, to recapture the coon-coated past.

Just before World War II he moved from Connecticut to Belmar, New Jersey, where after Pearl Harbor he served locally in the Army Signal Corps. When, in the fifties, another generation began to look back with a certain sentimental wistfulness to the manner of the twenties, Held tried to revive the bright and brittle dream of his lost midwestern campus. The impulse failed, and with it Held himself. He died in 1958. In a sense his failure was that of his sheiks and shebas who, gaily unprepared, had to learn suddenly the most ancient of lessons—that time is fleeting, that winter always follows autumn, and that whatever the next spring may bring, it is always another season.

Thirty years of "Progress" . . . as the old Life *saw them (on the left, Mr. Gibson's charmer, gone, gone, like Sheba herself)*

OLD *Life*

Letters from Denmark

The purpose of a written alphabet is to be legible. But why not play with it? Medieval scribes did. So does Peter Soederlund of Copenhagen, a designer familiar with all that's new in typography, yet who in these sample initials chooses to ignore it. Earlier in this issue, two Finnish designers, the Wirkkalas, are represented by their work in the most advanced taste; but not all Scandinavians are modern all the time.